CHARLES PHILLIPS

STAY
SMART

100 exercises to keep your brain sharp

CONNECTIONS
BOOK PUBLISHING

Charles Phillips would like to dedicate this book to his parents, David and Gay.

A CONNECTIONS EDITION
This edition published in Great Britain in 2012 by
Connections Book Publishing Limited,
St Chad's House, 148 King's Cross Road, London WC1X 9DH
www.connections-publishing.com

Text and puzzles copyright © Bibelot Limited 2012
This edition copyright © Eddison Sadd Editions 2012

The right of Charles Phillips to be identified as the author of the work has been asserted
by him in accordance with the Copyright, Designs and Patents Act 1988.

ISBN 978-1-85906-344-6

1 3 5 7 9 10 8 6 4 2

Phototypeset in Gill Sans and Interstate using InDesign on Apple Macintosh

Printed in Singapore

CONTENTS

INTRODUCTION

Have you ever had to pause in midsentence, unable to remember the name of a friend? Perhaps you've had a "senior moment" in which you've forgotten where you put your keys or muddled up the steps in a long-familiar dance routine. If you're getting older you may feel you're in decline. That time is against you.

But you'd be wrong to feel despondent. Because in recent years—largely through the use of functional magnetic resonance imaging (fMRI) and other high-tech approaches that enable technicians to show the brain in action—neuroscientists have greatly increased our knowledge of how this small, soft, but massively powerful organ works. And their highly encouraging report is that if we stay healthy and keep ourselves mentally active, there is usually no reason why brain and memory will not carry on performing well into our later years.

OLDER … BUT NO LESS SMART On average, society is growing older, with more and more people living to a ripe old age. For many decades, the conventional wisdom was that the brain and its performance were in decline from a person's 20s onwards and that there was no avoiding a falling away in mental functioning, in some cases to quite a severe extent.

Certainly brain changes do take place as we age. The brain communicates by sending electrical signals along nerve fibers insulated by a fatty material called myelin. As you age, your quantity of myelin falls away and the signals travel more slowly. There is less efficient communication between different parts of the brain, the blood supply to your brain drops, and the number of brain cells declines. As a result, the brain loses some volume—in other words, it becomes smaller. Some people—but by no means all—may also be affected by neurodegenerative disorders such as Alzheimer's disease.

But there is now strong evidence that the brain carries on adapting—and renewing itself—long into our later years.

7

For one thing, as we grow older the brain uses more of its areas in order to maintain performance; research shows that keeping the brain active counters the natural changes of aging so effectively that many people simply do not notice any of the effects.

It's even the case that in some respects—for example, the ability to manage our emotions and to see a problem in context—our flexible brain performs better in middle and old age than it does in youth. The evidence suggests that as we age our brain becomes more cheerful!

STAYING CONNECTED The key thing for brain performance is not the number of cells we have but the number and quality of connections between them. In the brain we have not only a very large number of neurons (one type of brain cell) but also an almost unimaginably large number of potential connections among them: There are 100 billion neurons and a potential 100 trillion connections.

The brain makes connections among its neurons when we learn new skills or information, when we ensure that we are engaged by what we do, and when we are mentally stimulated. Remain mentally active and you help protect yourself against the effects of natural decline.

A key study carried out with 4,000 nuns in Minnesota, U.S.A., beginning in 1991, showed that the sisters who kept active mentally, by carrying on with their teaching work into old age, had an average of 40 percent more brain connections than their fellow nuns who opted for a lower-stimulus lifestyle. And the industrious nuns lived four years longer on average than the less busy sisters. In fact, research published in 2006 at the University of New South Wales, Australia, showed that people who kept themselves mentally active through work and leisure, or by using brain-training games and puzzles, were half as likely as others to develop dementia.

We can maintain the brain's performance and help protect its future health by trying new and challenging activities, by making an effort to stay socially connected, by taking steps to be alert and retain an interest in what we do, and by attempting puzzles and challenges of the kind collected in this book.

MEMORY FUNCTION There is no one part of the brain that houses the memory. Instead, memory is a function performed by many parts of the brain working together. Research shows that the hippocampus in the brain's limbic system plays a key role in laying down new memories; the pre-frontal and frontal lobes in the forepart of your upper brain are important for managing facts learned through the conscious memory.

But what is most important from our perspective is to identify practical steps to safeguard and improve memory performance.

Thinking about memory function in three stages will help us focus on ways to boost performance: In the first stage you input material into your memory; in the second you keep it there; and in the third you recall the information when you need it.

When inputting material, make sure you are concentrating. This sounds obvious, but more often than we might like to admit we forget things because we weren't concentrating when we committed them to memory. In addition, try to process material as much as possible; make connections to diverse areas of the brain. Produce lists. Create visual images for facts and try to link these to sounds and sensations and even smells.

To safeguard and improve your brain's capacity to store information, do all you can to look after its health. Eat a brain-healthy diet (see page 10). Take regular exercise and be sure to get enough sleep.

To improve your powers of recall, try not to be anxious about your memory. Research shows that a small amount of stress can actually help people perform better when remembering but that significant amounts of worry make it much harder to remember. Here, too, it's important for you to make sure you get enough sleep.

Try also to limit distractions. You'll find you benefit from working on your concentration: Do puzzles and exercises or start a meditation program. Sometimes it can help to recreate the circumstances in which you input the facts. Emotions can also boost recall—try to recall how you felt when you were learning the material.

LET'S GET STARTED ... *Stay Smart* contains a wealth of puzzles and thinking challenges that will help exercise your memory and improve your powers of recall. These are supplemented, page by page, with Smart Brain Facts that expand on the information in this introduction, and Smart Brain Actions—small but powerful exercises to engage the brain, then further stretch and work the memory.

The answer section at the back contains supplementary information and occasional extra challenges as well as full solutions and, where necessary, explanations. There's so much packed into this small book. So why not turn the page and begin exploring …

A brain-healthy diet

Make sure you eat plenty of vegetables, fruits, cereals, healthy oils, and fish. You're free, if you wish, to enjoy alcohol in small amounts, but you should limit your intake of dairy foods. This "Mediterranean diet" has been shown to safeguard brain health and prevent the onset of dementia. Berries are a brain-boosting food: Recent research suggests that blueberry juice and purple grape juice have benefits.

EASY
BRAIN TEASERS

The Roman philosopher and statesman Cicero
declared that memory is the "treasure house and
guard of all things." A master of rhetoric, he could
speak without notes for three hours. And you can
set out to follow in his footsteps with our recall
challenges and tests of numerical and spatial logic.
To begin with, warm up with the easier challenges
in this first section.

STAY SMART PUZZLE 1

OCTAPLUS

Can you correctly enter eight numbers into the diagram in line with the octaclues below? Note that no two numbers are the same; and all are whole numbers with a value no lower than 2 and no greater than 35.

1 F minus C is either 24 or 25.
2 G is a square number.
3 C is one-third of E; it's also half of G.
4 A minus D equals H.

5 B multiplied by C equals E.
6 One quarter of G equals D.
7 E divided by D equals A.
8 F divided by H equals G.

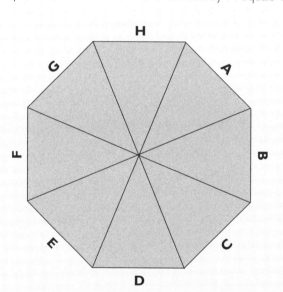

SMART BRAIN FACT

Puzzling protects your memory. A 2009 study led by the Albert Einstein College of Medicine in New York indicated that people who did a mental exercise such as a puzzle twice a day delayed memory loss linked to dementia.

STAY SMART PUZZLE 2

ARITHMETEST

Here's a quick test for your speed of arithmetic. Do these calculations as fast as you can. Take a watch with a second hand or use the stopwatch function on your smartphone or computer to time yourself. Try to beat the suggested time limit of 1 minute.

As you go through them, write your answers on a sheet of paper or on the Notes and Scribbles pages at the back of the book, so that you can return after a few days to do them again. You could even do them a third or fourth time later on. This kind of mental work-out improves your attentiveness and sharpens your short-term memory.

A	B	C
5 + 3 =	9 + 4 =	11 − 8 =
6 + 5 =	4 × 8 =	21 ÷ 7 =
18 ÷ 3 =	32 − 23 =	31 + 6 =
3 + 9 =	20 ÷ 5 =	44 ÷ 11 =
17 − 8 =	4 × 3 =	11 − 7 =
12 ÷ 3 =	3 + 5 =	5 − 3 =
22 − 7 =	8 ÷ 4 =	42 ÷ 7 =
9 × 7 =	12 × 5 =	13 × 3 =
29 − 13 =	13 − 8 =	11 + 6 =
7 × 8 =	14 + 13 =	21 + 11 =

SMART BRAIN ACTION

Visualize facts you are trying to remember. Imagine you're at a conference and meet three clients: Sandy, Arturo, and Anthony. Try to come up with three visual images that help you peg their names in your memory.

AROUND THE WORLD

Mnemonics are a handy way of committing dry facts to memory. Well-known examples encode the first letters of the colors of the rainbow: red, orange, yellow, green, blue, indigo, violet. One is the name Roy G. Biv. Another, used in Britain, is "Richard of York gave battle in vain" and refers to Richard, Duke of York's defeat in the Battle of Wakefield on December 30, 1460. One familiar to musicians records the sequence of notes in the spaces of a treble clef, E,G,B,D,F: "Every Good Boy Deserves Favor."

Your challenge here is to see if you can remember the following:

The names of the world's continents?
The names of its five oceans?

Can you invent a good mnemonic to encode them?

If you create visual images or other sensual associations for the mnemonics they will be more memorable still.

As a follow-up challenge, can you think of a catchy mnemonic to help you remember the top five countries with the longest coastlines: Canada, Indonesia, Greenland, Russia, and the Philippines?

SMART BRAIN FACT

Each second an astounding 100,000 chemical reactions take place in your brain. The electrical impulse sent by a neuron lasts 1/1,000th of a second and travels at speeds of up to 200 mph (320 km/hour).

STAY SMART PUZZLE 4

MEMORY BOX

A long-lost schoolfriend sends you this chart, which gives directions to a hidden "memory box" containing everyday items from your childhood. The box is behind the central dark square in the grid: To arrive there, you have to move the indicated number of spaces north, south, east, and west —for example, 3W means move three squares west. You must stop once only at every square. Can you work out at which square you should start?

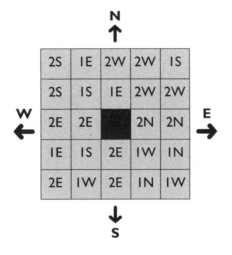

	N ↑		

2S	IE	2W	2W	IS
2S	IS	IE	2W	2W
2E	2E	■	2N	2N
IE	IS	2E	IW	IN
2E	IW	2E	IN	IW

W ←   E →

S ↓

SMART BRAIN ACTION

Can you commit this list of soccer greats to memory? John Charles, Pele, Dino Zoff, Eric Cantona, Lionel Messi, Roberto Baggio, Ferenc Puskas, Stan Bowles, Ronaldo, Johan Cruyff, Paolo Maldini, Liam Brady, George Best? Try reading them aloud to see if that helps.

STAY SMART PUZZLE 5

POLYGON OVERLAY

Here your task is to work out the logic behind the numbers in these shapes, and then calculate the total of B divided by A. This kind of puzzle is good as a mental warm-up and helps sharpen your thinking: Working your brain in this way makes you more likely to perform well when faced with a memory test.

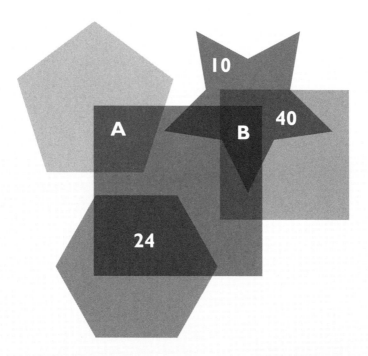

SMART BRAIN FACT

In your brain, signals travel from one neuron to another along a long tendril (axon), then across a tiny gap (synapse). Chemicals (neurotransmitters) carry the signal across the gap, and threads (dendrites) receive the signal. There are at least 100 known neurotransmitters.

STAY SMART PUZZLE 6

COGITATION

Let your mind take a turn around this problem: Cog A has eight teeth, cog B has seven, and cog C has fourteen. How many revolutions must Cog A turn through to bring all three cogs back to these exact positions?

This is the kind of thinking challenge that I recommend for getting your mental wheels turning—like Polygon Overlay, opposite, it's great for developing speed and clarity of thought and in turn boosting memory performance.

SMART BRAIN ACTION

Commit this sequence of numbers to memory: 4181994263253. Try this technique: Convert the alphabet into numbers (A = 1, B = 2, etc.) then think of celebrities or fictional characters: 819 HS could be Homer Simpson, and so on.

STAY SMART PUZZLE 7
COLOR OVERRIDE

As discussed in the introduction, your memory performance depends to a significant degree on how focused your attention is. You need to be paying full attention whether you're inputting material into your memory or trying to recall facts.

Here's a great test for your alertness. It's called the Stroop Test after the American psychologist John Ridley Stroop (1897–1973), who was the first writer in English to note the effect it tests, in 1935. (It had previously been described in German in the late 1920s.)

This exercise works as a test of how focused you are and as a way of sharpening your powers of concentration.

First you need to get hold of some colored pens or crayons. Then take a sheet of paper or turn to the Notes and Scribbles pages. Near the top write the words RED, GREEN, BLUE, and BLACK in their correct colors. Beneath, on the next line, write them again, in the correct color but in a different order. Then write them (in any order) in the wrong colors, for example, write RED in green ink and BLUE in black ink. Do this five more times until you have eight lines of words.

Now read out the list as quickly as you can. But don't say the words, say the color in which the words are written. You have to override your impulse to read the word and instead process then name the color.

SMART BRAIN FACT

You've heard of your "gray matter?" This is actually your neurons. The connecting axons and dendrites described in the Smart Brain Fact on page 16 are what we call your "white matter."

STAY SMART PUZZLE 8
DIGITAL SEQUENCING

Which of the four alternatives provided below—A, B, C, or D—replicates the pattern in the first three number squares in the top sequence? Look for sequences among the digits in the boxes. As we saw in the introduction, stimulating the brain promotes the growth of new brain cells and of new connections among these cells—which safeguards your brain's future health and the continuing good performance of your memory.

15	17	20
24	29	35
42	50	59

12	14	17
21	26	32
39	47	56

17	19	22
26	31	37
44	52	61

?

13	15	18
22	27	33
40	49	57

A

11	13	16
20	25	31
38	46	55

B

16	19	21
25	30	36
43	51	60

C

14	16	19
24	28	34
41	49	58

D

SMART BRAIN ACTION

Commit these salad foods to memory in sequence. Try visualizing each as a celebrity/ fictional character (see page 17) or as a friend or family member: Cos lettuce, tomato, scallion, celery, radicchio, spinach, rocket, cucumber, radish.

STAY SMART PUZZLE 9

HONEYCOMB LINKS

This puzzle—like Lighten Up, opposite, and many other challenges in this book—maintains and improves your memory by working the brain and in particular developing positional logic. Some of the circles in this puzzle are already shaded. Shade in more white circles, so that the number of shaded circles totals the number inside the area they surround. One rule applies: Every shaded circle surrounding an area with a number higher than "1" needs to be next to another shaded circle. When solving, it may help to put a small dot into any circle you know should not be filled.

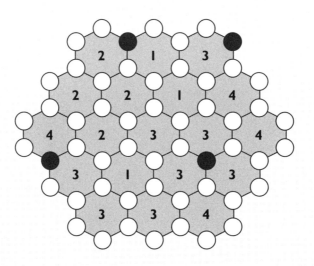

SMART BRAIN FACT

Brain scientists distinguish between short- and long-term memory. We store information for a few minutes or hours in the short-term memory, but to recall facts in a few days, weeks, or even years they have to be transferred to the long-term memory.

STAY SMART PUZZLE 10
LIGHTEN UP

In this puzzle, circles represent light bulbs. A bulb sends rays of light horizontally and vertically (but not diagonally), illuminating its entire row and column unless its light is blocked by a dark cell. Your task is to place bulbs in empty squares so that no two bulbs shine on each other, until the entire grid is lit up.

Some dark cells contain numbers, indicating how many light bulbs are in squares either above, below, to the right, or to the left. Bulbs placed diagonally adjacent to a numbered cell do not contribute to the bulb count. An unnumbered dark cell may have any number of light bulbs adjacent to it, or none at all, and not all light bulbs are necessarily clued via dark squares.

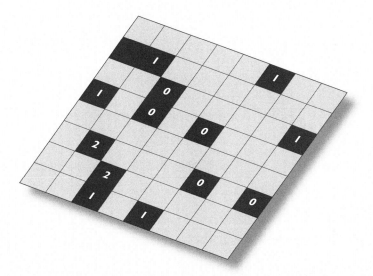

SMART BRAIN ACTION

Codebreaking challenges improve concentration, bringing benefits to overall memory performance. Try this elementary challenge: If Slonvh is Holmes, who are Klrilg, Nzikov, and Drnhvb? I think Sherlock might give Watson a clue about the need to think backward.

STAY SMART PUZZLE 11

SACRED REPETITION

The priests of the Ancient Indian Vedic culture around 3,500 years ago developed powerful memorization techniques for learning—and passing down through the generations—the hymns of their Rig Veda scripture.

One of these techniques was called *jatapatha* ("enmeshed reciting"). They memorized a line like this: AB, BA, AB; BC, CB, BC … and so on. To learn the line "We meditate on the beautiful light of the sun god Savitri. May this light enliven our thinking," they would begin: "We meditate, meditate we, we meditate, meditate on, on meditate, meditate on, on the …"

Another was called *ghanapatha* ("dense text"). In this the repetition followed the pattern, AB, BA, ABC, CBA, BC, CB, BCD, DBC: "We meditate, meditate we, we meditate on, on meditate we, meditate on, on meditate, meditate on the, the on meditate …"

Try out these techniques to learn the following lines. Try simply repeating the first two lines to commit them to memory, then use *jatapatha* to memorize the next two lines, and *ghanapatha* to learn the final two lines. Do you notice any benefit from using these Ancient Indian techniques?

LINES

1 The scrubby, under-watered headland
2 Is hit by an unforgiving wind
3 Which today comes hot off yellow hills
4 And with no hint
5 Of an endless blue-beautiful sea
6 Unseen less than a mile away.

SMART BRAIN FACT

Memory experts report that most of us can hold only 5–9 units in the short-term memory at a time. This insight is useful in memory training: To help you remember a longer number, try "chunking" it—breaking it into chunks of 3–5 digits.

NUMBER STEP

Here's another test of spatial-sequential logic to develop the visualization skills so important in memory performance.

This time your task is to place the digits 1–9 in the grid so that it's possible to jump from one digit to the next, in order, using the steps provided. (For example, the 2 and 1 in the upper-left diamond piece mean two steps left, one step up.) Each step must be used once. Both parts of a step must be used but can be taken in any order. No part of a step can be over a dark square.

SMART BRAIN ACTION

Read these long numbers three times, then cover the book and try to recall them. Before you start, remember the benefits of "chunking" (dividing into sections of 3–5 numbers): 17783451511; 67651326912; 37854322586.

STAY SMART PUZZLE 13
NUMBER LADDERS

A capacity for quick thinking and a facility with numbers, both developed by our Number Ladders puzzle, are key attributes for your memory function. Your task is to start with the figure given then follow the sums from the top to the bottom of each Number Ladder to work out the two answers.

EASY	TOUGH
3	**3**
Multiply by 8	Add 78
Divide by 2	Divide by 9
Add 23	Add 55
Divide by 5	Divide by 16
Multiply by 6	Add 24
Divide by 2	Divide by 4
Divide by 7	Multiply by 9
Multiply by 6	Subtract 15
Divide by 2	Divide by 12
ANSWER	ANSWER

SMART BRAIN FACT

You have 100 billion neurons but these are outnumbered 10 to 1 by glial cells. Scientists once thought glial cells merely held the brain together, but we now know they play a key role, supporting and sustaining the brain, and strengthening neural signals.

STAY SMART PUZZLE 14
GET IN SHAPE

Can you fill up the box so that each row, column, and long diagonal contains four different shapes and all the letters A, B, C, and D? A puzzle like this drives activity in diverse brain regions by making you balance spatial thinking with a focus on letters and on simple polygons. This builds brain connections, precisely what you need to boost the memory and maintain your overall mental performance.

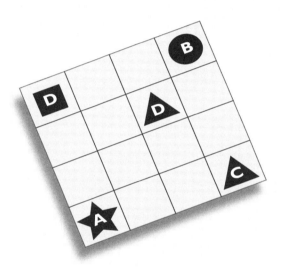

SMART BRAIN ACTION

You must remember how to do this! In this anagram challenge, can you untangle the names Gindir Gambern, Phurmhey Grobat, and Ludace Niras and tell me what links them?

STAY SMART PUZZLE 15

MEMORY WALK

The Ancient Greeks bequeathed to us a memory technique later called "the method of loci," from Latin *locus* meaning "place." First visualize a room or building you know well and imagine a walk through it past a series of places. Next take the material you want to memorize and choose visual symbols to represent its different elements. Then place these visual symbols in the places within your memory house. When you want to recall the facts, imagine yourself making the walk and encountering the symbols one by one.

For this exercise, think of a walk you know well. This could be the walk from the station to your workplace, or from your house to the nearest shops, or a walk you take for pleasure in a park or area of countryside.

Now choose eleven places on the walk and use these to visualize this list of the main bones of the body's upper half. Be as imaginative as you can. For example, a crane (machine or bird) for cranium, a man for mandible, perhaps a little ("ickle") shell for "clavicle," and so on.

MAIN BONES Cranium, Mandible, Clavicle, Manubrium, Scapula, Sternum, Ribs, Humerus, Vertebrae, Radius, Ulna

SMART BRAIN FACT

If your brain were a computer it would have a capacity of 1,000,000,000,000 (a trillion) gigabytes. This figure was worked out by Jeff Lichtman of the Center for Brain Science at Harvard University.

STAY SMART PUZZLE 16
DIGITAL HUBS

As we've seen previously, you need to be alert, focused, and mentally engaged to get the best out of your memory.

This Digital Hubs challenge develops your clarity of thinking and confidence with numbers. Your task is to work out the missing number from the center of Hub B. To do this, study the relationships between the numbers in Hub A and apply them to Hub B.

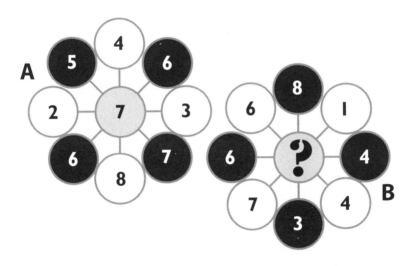

SMART BRAIN ACTION

Count aloud in 4s to 100. Then do it backward. Or perform simple calculations—such as [(2 x 3 x 5 x 2) ÷ 10] x 3—quickly. If you repeat exercises like this regularly it will improve your numerical facility and memory.

STAY SMART PUZZLE 17

FLAGS UNITED

You've been offered a week's work in an important embassy, but to be selected you have to prove your short-term memory is up to scratch by acing this test. Your task is to study this grid of flags, then cover it up to answer the questions below. Grab a sheet of paper or turn to the Notes and Scribbles pages to record your answers.

1   How many stars are there in the grid?
2   Is the highest-placed cross in the grid white or dark?
3   How many unique flags are there in the grid?
4   Where is the twin flag to the first one in the second row?
5   Twin flags occupy spots 1 and 4 in which row?
6   Column 4 row 4 has what shape on a white background?
7   Flag 1, row 2 has how many dark horizontal stripes?
8   How many stars are there in the bottom row?
9   Are all the flags in column 3 different?
10 Where is the flag with the smallest star?

SMART BRAIN FACT

A ten-year study at Pittsburgh University reported in 2010 that patients who walked 6 miles (9.5 km) a week had larger brains, better memories, and less chance of developing dementia than those who were less active.

DOWNTOWN PARKING

Three dark limousines heading for an important meeting of Mafia families are entering the Downtown district, where there are three available garages: A, B, and C. The three sets of directions below will each take one limo to one garage, but which one and to which garage?

This puzzle provides practice in both logical thinking and visual plotting, and, like Puzzle 17, it works your short-term memory.

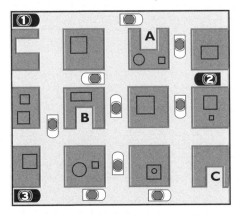

DIRECTIONS
  i Take the third right, then first right, first right again, second right, and turn right.

  ii Take the first left, then second right, then second left, left, and turn left.

  iii Take the second turning on the right, then second left, first right, first left, and turn left.

SMART BRAIN ACTION

Read this list of writers and dramatists twice, then close the book and repeat them in the order printed here: Charles Dickens, Christopher Marlowe, George Orwell, Henry Fielding, George Eliot, D.H. Lawrence, John Fletcher, Jane Austen, Ben Jonson.

STAY SMART PUZZLE 19
A TASTE OF REMEMBERING

The French author Marcel Proust is best known for the account in his novel *Remembrance of Things Past* of how tasting a "madeleine" (a small cake) soaked in tea transported him directly and powerfully back to his childhood holiday experiences. You can use this effect to make it easier to remember facts by recreating the sensory conditions in which you learned them.

Test the theory. Try to commit to memory this list of British trees. While you do so, breathe in a perfume or odor of your choice—a piece of fruit, some fine soap, a palmful of herbs, eau de cologne, or bottled perfume … Close or cover the book and take a break, then try to recall the trees while again smelling the perfume or odor you chose.

TREES   Alder, Sweet Chestnut, Elder, Ash, Rowan, Juniper, Whitebeam, Hawthorn, Plane, Buckthorn, Hornbeam

Now try with a taste. Attempt to memorize this list of North American trees. While you do so, eat or drink something with a notable taste—dark chocolate, a banana, some peanuts, or strong black coffee … As before, close or cover the book and take a break, then try to recall the trees while tasting again the flavor you chose.

TREES   Quaking aspen, Douglas fir, American chestnut, White ash, Red alder, Northern white cedar, California red fir, Paper birch, American basswood, Monterey cypress

SMART BRAIN FACT

The human brain weighs just 3 lb (1.4 kg) but uses up to 20 percent of the body's energy. Most of this energy is consumed by the firing of your millions of neurons as they communicate.

STAY SMART PUZZLE 20

ADD-UPS

Try doing these pyramid Add-ups as quickly as you can. The design is simple: In each pyramid, the number in a circle is the sum of the two numbers in the circles underneath it; your task is to fill in the empty circles to complete the pyramids. Can you do all three in under 60 seconds?

Here is an extra challenge: Imagine the three pyramids are the three faces of a triangular-based pyramid: What would the total be of all the second-row numbers? What is special about this number?

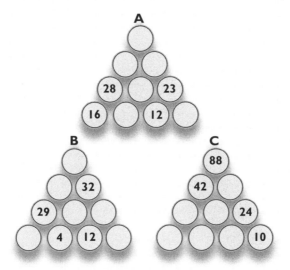

SMART BRAIN ACTION

Learn these five names: Jermaine McCalla, Augustus Wilson, Rowan Phillips, Randy Green, Armand P. Silvester. Connect the names to your senses: Say or sing them, create visual images, touch or smell. After 1 minute, close the book and try to write them in order.

STAY SMART PUZZLE 21
NEAT FIT

When you're committing material to memory you benefit from having a sure eye for how it fits together. In this spatial challenge, your task is to divide the grid into rectangles so that each rectangle contains a single digit that indicates the number of boxes within the rectangle.

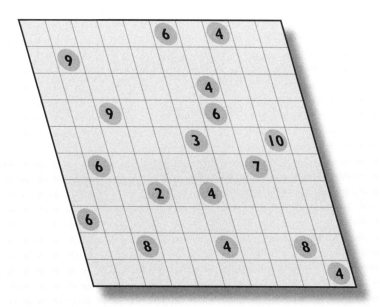

SMART BRAIN FACT

The brain makes new neurons (brain cells) throughout your life. This process, called neurogenesis, was first demonstrated as recently as 1998; previously, scientists had thought that the brain cells you were born with were the only ones you'd ever have.

STAY SMART PUZZLE 22

HEXAGON TWIST

Like Neat Fit, opposite, this puzzle develops your visual–spatial facility while testing and building your concentration in order to bring focus to your memory function. Here you're required to rotate the five hexagons so that all of the neighboring panels match up.

SMART BRAIN ACTION

To help you memorize this shopping list divide it into categories, alphabetically or by food type or by likes/dislikes: pears, milk, salt beef, brown bread, butter, beetroot, plums, leeks, crackers, liver, carrots, pomegranate juice, peanuts, potatoes, spaghetti, tomatoes.

STAY SMART PUZZLE 23
FRACTION STATIONS

Working on quickfire puzzles like this reminds you of the need to be accurate; of course, your ability to recall facts or numbers is completely undermined if you're careless when you learn them. Here your task is to determine what fraction of the tiles in this design is white and what percentage is dark purple.

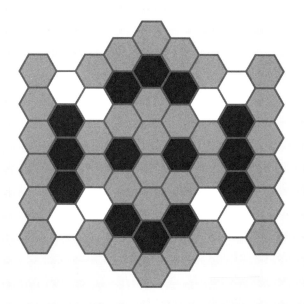

SMART BRAIN FACT

Research shows that emotional engagement boosts memory performance. You remember facts better if you feel strongly about them or have an emotional pull to remember. You can also try to "fix" facts by summoning strong emotions.

STAY SMART PUZZLE 24

GET IN CHARACTER

Top actors long to play Hamlet. The fact that the "Dane" has around 1,500 lines—more than any other Shakespearean character in a single play—doesn't put them off.

You might think that, having got the part, the actors would set aside days or even weeks to learn all these lines. But many actors report that they don't actually learn lines by rote. Instead they concentrate on what the words mean and on the motivation of their character, moment by moment, throughout the play. And they make sure they understand their character's response to every other person in a scene.

The iconic British actor Michael Caine said, "You must be able to stand there not thinking of [your] line. You take it off the other actor's face."

Can you apply this insight to learning a poem? Choose any poem you like but don't already know by heart. Concentrate on the situation or story and on the desire and needs of the narrating voice or of any characters in the poem.

SMART BRAIN ACTION

Trying to memorize a stanza or lyric each day builds your confidence with words and short-term memory. If you have an interest in religion, learn a scriptural passage, hymn, or uplifting prayer. You'll be able to impress people by quoting Shakespeare or the great poets.

STAY SMART PUZZLE 25
NUMBER NEST

This puzzle combines simple arithmetic with spatial logic; as we have seen, tasks that work diverse brain areas are good for thinking and benefit the memory function.

Place the values 0–9 into the number nest so that they appear once in a white hexagon and once in a dark hexagon. Values of white hexagons must equal the sum of the values of the surrounding dark hexagons. If these values add up to a two-digit number, place the second digit in the white hexagon. For example : 4 + 5 + 3 = 12; place 2 in the hexagon.

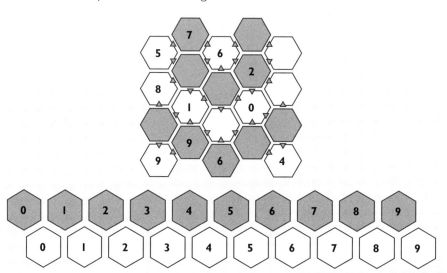

SMART BRAIN FACT

Eating spinach, broccoli, and other magnesium-rich foods boosts the memory and brain performance, according to 2010 research at Tsinghua University, Beijing. In industrialized countries, though, only half of us get enough magnesium in our diets.

PICTURE THIS

A tried and tested memory strategy is to link data to memorable visual images. One useful technique is to think of a striking image for each of the numbers from 0–9. Then, when you're trying to commit a number to memory, imagine a picture or narrative combining the images.

Say you link 3 to a pair of bulbous eyes and 9 to an old-fashioned monocle on a string, then 39 could be a man lifting a monocle in front of his eyes …
4 could be the sail in a yacht and 7 the side of an ocean liner, so 74 could be a *Titanic*-sized liner heading toward a vulnerable-looking yacht.

This technique works best if you make your own choice of number images and then take time to draw them. Turn to the Notes and Scribbles pages now and draw your images for 0–9. Then come up with images or small stories for the numbers shown below.

Come back to this in a couple of days and see how well you can remember the images/stories—and the numbers.

> 4,732
> 961,267

SMART BRAIN ACTION

Linguistic puzzles benefit memory and other areas of thinking. Can you solve this simple riddle? My third comes right after A, and a river runs through me that starts with my fourth. I am famous for a dark drink. What is my name?

CRISS-CROSS

Making sure you face a mental challenge every day is a good way to preserve your brain performance and the functioning of your memory. You may get this from your job, but not all jobs provide mental engagement and if you are retired you may need to plan to include a challenge in your day. Crosswords or puzzles are one option.

This is an engaging numberfit game. Place the numbers 1–9 in each row. Numbers may appear multiple times in columns. Identical numbers may not appear in neighboring squares (even diagonally). Some diagonal totals are provided around the outside of the grid.

	11	31		27	12			
	4			8	7	9		5
		8	6	2	3			
35 → 2		4			1			3 ← 25
7			5	9	4		8	2
22 →			4	2	1			6 ← 16
		8		9	4	2	1	5
6 →			7		8	9		2 ← 9
5	3		8				1	
7		4		9		5	3	

SMART BRAIN FACT

More active brains may be better able to compensate for physical damage (caused by, for example, injury, stroke, or dementia). People with active brains develop "cognitive reserve" (a back-up of neural network and mental processing power).

STAY SMART PUZZLE 28
TEN FINGER FACTS—AT THE MOVIES!

We've all heard of finger foods, but what are finger facts? If you link data you're trying to learn to your fingers, looking at or counting through the fingers should help you recall the facts. Of course you can apply this technique to other body parts.

Try committing the names of these movie directors to memory, using one finger for each. (Some are very well known, others less so to make this more of a challenge …)

DIRECTORS   Joanna Hogg, Alfred Hitchcock, Kelly Reichardt, Frank Capra, Peter Bogdanovich, Steven Spielberg, Lisa Cholodenko, Vittorio De Sica, Zhang Yimou, Woody Allen

Thumbs, fingers, action! Run through the fingers (and names) three times, in order. Now try to take the fingers (and names) in random order. Then cover the book and try writing the names on a piece of paper. Take a 5-minute break. Write the names again. Use your fingers to aid recall.

One more thing: You have to get the spellings right!

SMART BRAIN ACTION

If you often lose everyday items, this simple practical step may help—create a "memory place" in your house or apartment to store keys, wallet, or TV remote. You can also drop notes there reminding yourself of tasks or ideas.

STAY SMART PUZZLE 29
TAKE YOUR PLACE

An ability to see context and the overall picture is a key attribute when familiarizing yourself with material you need to commit to memory. This puzzle and Building Blocks, opposite, are focused on this ability.

The design of the Take Your Place grid follows a logical pattern. Your task is to study the layout to determine which designs should be placed in the empty squares A, B, and C.

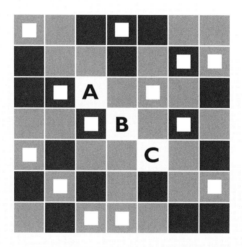

SMART BRAIN FACT

An active brain may slow the onset of some brain diseases. Post-mortems have shown that some people with Alzheimer's-style brain degeneration had no symptoms at all: By being mentally active they had countered the effects.

STAY SMART PUZZLE 30

BUILDING BLOCKS

Which two of these block piles could be fitted neatly together to make a perfect 3x3x3 cube?

In addition to testing your ability to see the overall picture, this type of puzzle develops your capacity to visualize shapes in three dimensions.

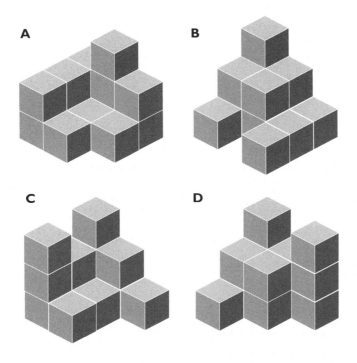

A   B

C   D

SMART BRAIN ACTION

Try this diary code. The answers to these three sums encode three dates written as xx/xx/xx, in the month/date/year format. 61,557 x 2; 861,570 − 761,459; 791,091 ÷ 7. What are the dates?

STAY SMART PUZZLE 31

MATH ODDITY

Solve this multiplication problem and write the numerical answer into the top set of boxes below the line. Then use the decoder to the left of the sum, writing the letters into the boxes beneath the numbers in order to find a name. This develops your ability to process information quickly and accurately.

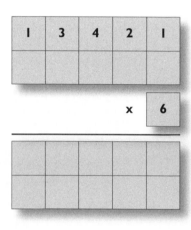

0	O
1	D
2	I
3	A
4	V
5	W
6	E
7	R
8	B
9	S

1	3	4	2	1

x 6

SMART BRAIN FACT

The largest part of your brain is the cerebrum, divided into right and left hemispheres. The right is involved more in spatial judgment and awareness of your body, the left more in language and speech.

STAY SMART PUZZLE 32
ONCE UPON A TIME

When you have a list of things you need to remember, try connecting them in a chain—perhaps by creating a story. As we've seen, you will find it easier to recall information if you process it in as many ways as possible—by categorizing it, linking it to images, smells, or sounds, or by chunking it into smaller sequences.

Use a story to dramatize and embed this shopping/to do list in your memory.

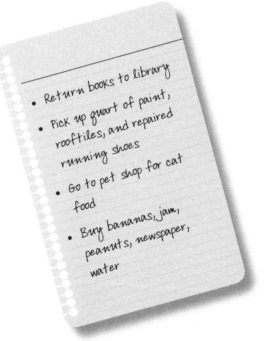

- Return books to library
- Pick up quart of paint, rooftiles, and repaired running shoes
- Go to pet shop for cat food
- Buy bananas, jam, peanuts, newspaper, water

SMART BRAIN ACTION

Engage your brain by setting yourself an occasional imaginative challenge. Where would I go and what would I do if I could travel instantly and freely? Which person from my childhood would I like to see today? Is there a product from my youth I'd like to see reintroduced?

STAY SMART PUZZLE 33
NAVIGATOR

This simple placement puzzle requires you to visualize spatial connections while processing directions accurately. In our Navigator puzzle every oval shape should contain a different letter of the alphabet from A–K inclusive. Use the clues below to determine the locations of the letters.

1 The B is farther north than the H, but farther south than the K (which is farther south than the G).
2 The D is next to and east of the J, which is farther south than the C.
3 The F is next to and south of the E, which is next to and west of the C.
4 The G is next to and north of the I, which is next to and west of the A.

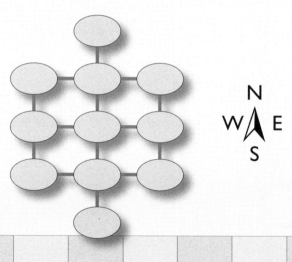

SMART BRAIN FACT

Increased folic acid intake improves memory and brain performance in older people, according to 2007 research at the University of Wageningen, Netherlands. (But care must be taken as too much can mask anemia symptoms.)

INTERMEDIATE MIND STRETCHERS

Shakespeare's Lady Macbeth called memory "the warder of the brain." So many of our mental processes, even our identity from day to day, depend on our short- and long-term memory; in taking steps to safeguard your memory performance, you are paying attention to who you are. By this stage of the book, you're ready to move on to the intermediate-level puzzles and challenges that stretch your powers of recall, visualization skills, and capacity for clear thinking a little further.

STAY SMART PUZZLE 34
DICE PATH

Hone your logical powers with our Dice Path puzzle. Each shade represents a direction (up, down, left, or right) and the number of dots on each die indicates how far to go. Starting from the middle die of the maze, follow the directions correctly and you will visit every die in turn once only.

Can you work out which shade represents which direction and determine which die is the last you visit on your trip?

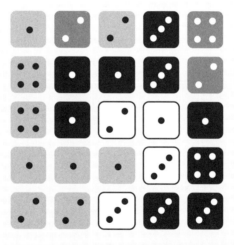

SMART BRAIN FACT

If you indulge in a heavy evening drinking alcohol at a party, you risk damaging your long-term memory because it impacts on the hippocampus, a brain region that's key to memory function.

STAY SMART PUZZLE 35
A BARD'S DOZEN

Can you memorize a list of twelve of William Shakespeare's plays? Study the list for 1 minute. Then turn to the Notes and Scribbles pages, or take a piece of paper, and write down as many as you can.

It will help you if you process the list in whichever way works for you: perhaps into history plays, tragedies, and comedies; or into one-word titles, titles beginning with "the," and others; or into titles you know well, others you know quite well, and the ones you have scarcely heard of.

PLAYS
- *The Two Gentlemen of Verona*
- *Macbeth*
- *Timon of Athens*
- *A Midsummer Night's Dream*
- *Henry VIII*
- *King John*
- *Hamlet*
- *Twelfth Night*
- *The Merchant of Venice*
- *Henry IV Part I*
- *Measure for Measure*
- *The Merry Wives of Windsor*

SMART BRAIN ACTION

When a fact's on the tip of your tongue, use the power of association. One technique is to run through the letters of the alphabet: Say you want to remember who starred in *The Night of the Hunter*, when you reach M you may recall "Mitchum—Robert Mitchum."

STAY SMART PUZZLE 36

BINGO MIX-UP

The bingo balls below have been rearranged so that they are in the same pattern but in different positions. Can you work out the new arrangement from the clues? With this exercise you will develop—and test—your capacity for deductive thinking.

CLUES
1 All of the balls have moved.
2 The top ball is still an even number.
3 The lowest two balls still add up to 7.
4 The 2 ball is not touching the 1 ball.

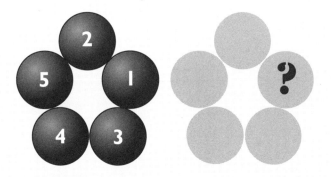

SMART BRAIN FACT

Research has shown that if you listen to a piano sonata (or lie on a sofa bed) when learning facts, listening to the same sonata (or lying in the same position) will help you recall them faster and more accurately.

STAY SMART PUZZLE 37
TAKING A TURN

Get your thinking cap on for a second chance at this toothy challenge (see Puzzle 6). Cog A has eight teeth, while Cog B has fourteen, and Cog C has sixteen. How many revolutions must Cog A turn through to bring all three cogs back to these exact starting positions?

This exercise develops your visual intelligence while working your facility with numbers.

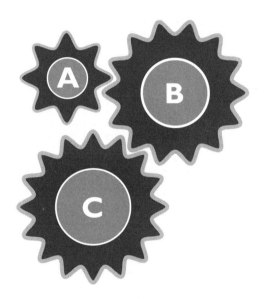

SMART BRAIN ACTION

If A = 1, B = 2, and so on, what's the sum total of Charles Dickens? In 30 seconds name five Dickens novels, including two made into movies and one made into a musical. And what's the total of the Dickens character Edwin Drood?

STAY SMART PUZZLE 38

NUMBER WAFFLE

Sharpen your mental focus and benefit your memory with this numerical logic grid. Can you discover the sixteen numbers that match all the clues below? All are whole numbers, no two are the same, and none has a value of less than 1 or more than 99. (Some numbers have been added to help you get started.)

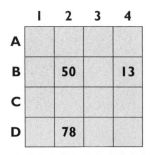

1. A1 is either A4 plus B3 or A4 minus B3.
2. A2 is three-sevenths of B3.
3. A3 is either C4 minus A4 or C4 plus A4.
4. A4 is either one ninth of D1 or nine times D1.
5. B1 is either 20 or 24.
6. B2 is either D2 minus B3 or D2 plus B3.
7. B3 is either B1 minus C2 or D3 plus C2.
8. B4 is one quarter of A3.
9. C1 is either A3 plus B4 or A3 minus B4.
10. C2 is one fifth of B1.
11. C3 is either D4 plus B4 or D4 minus B2.
12. C4 is either D3 minus A1 or D3 plus A1.
13. D1 is one quarter of A2.
14. D2 is either one third of C1 or double C1.
15. D3 is either B1 minus C2 or B1 plus C2.
16. D4 is either B2 plus B3 or B2 plus A4.

SMART BRAIN FACT

Eggs are a good brain food. They are rich in choline, used by the body to make the neurotransmitter acetylcholine, linked to good memory performance; low acetylcholine levels are connected to Alzheimer's disease.

STAY SMART PUZZLE 39
GRID SPLIT

Here's a second chance to work at a Shikaku grid (see Puzzle 21). As before, it's a simple test of logic, developing your eye for how parts combine in the whole: Divide the grid into rectangles so that each rectangle contains a single number indicating how many boxes there are in the rectangle.

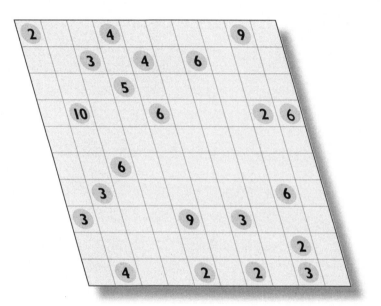

SMART BRAIN ACTION

Try to do this simple anagram challenge in less than a minute. Who are Lardon Garean, Rackab Maboa, Libl Nilcont, and Mymij Racret? Now try compiling some of your own to test out on friends, family, or co-workers.

STAY SMART PUZZLE 40
SHAPE STACKER

Here's a second opportunity to work at this decoding challenge (see Puzzle 5). As before, your job is to work out the logic behind the numbers in these shapes and then make a calculation—this time, A times B. The puzzle demands and develops accuracy and clear thinking.

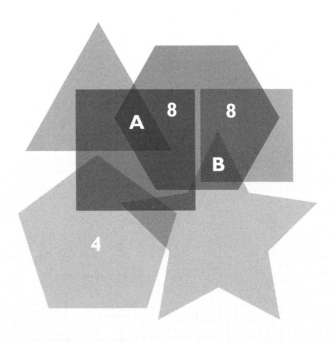

SMART BRAIN FACT

Is there something fishy about having a good memory? Research in 2009 suggested that taking fish oil supplements improved memory in those beginning to suffer age-related memory loss.

STEP BY STEP

Take another turn at descending our number ladders (see Puzzle 13). Go as fast as you can while maintaining accuracy. As before, you start with the number given, then follow the sums from top to bottom to reach two answers. What are the answers?

EASY	TOUGH
6	**17**
Add 66	Multiply by 3
Divide by 9	Add 117
Add 128	Divide by 14
Divide by 4	Halve it
Subtract 18	Cube it
Divide by 4	Divide by 8
Treble it	Divide by 3
Treble it	Add 333
Divide by 6	Divide by 18
ANSWER	ANSWER

SMART BRAIN ACTION

Can you come up with a mnemonic to help you remember the tallest mountains on the continents of Asia, South America, North America, Africa, Europe, and Antarctica: Everest, Aconcagua, McKinley, Kilimanjaro, Elbrus, and Vinson?

STAY SMART PUZZLE 42
"I CAN SEE IT NOW"

People tend to be good at remembering visual prompts. When you have to commit facts or names to memory, try creating visual images to fix them in your mind's eye and make them easier to recall. If you're introduced to key clients called Mr. Gregg, Ms. Walker, and Ms. Ash, you could visualize a giant egg, a walking boot, and a tree (or a cigarette butt). Images don't need to be polite—they're often more memorable if they're not. To generate ideas, think of what names sound like.

Now imagine you're taking a seminar and have to memorize the names of nine participants in short order. Here are the names:

NAMES   George, Sunil, Nelson, Amelia, Taiwo, Isaac, Wayne, Jermaine, Tom

Create visual images for the names and commit them to memory. After 2 minutes close the book, take a sheet of paper, and write them all down in order.

SMART BRAIN FACT

The Latin rhetoric handbook *Rhetorica ad Herennium* (85 BCE) distinguished between natural and artificial memory. The first is the inbuilt capacity to learn and remember; the second can be developed with memory techniques.

STAY SMART PUZZLE 43
MIDNIGHT HIVE

Look closely at our beehive: you'll see that some cells are occupied by sleeping bees (eyes closed) while others are buzzing with energy (eyes open). Demonstrate your numerical intelligence and engage your working memory to determine what fraction of the honeycomb is occupied by slumbering bees, and what fraction is occupied by bees both asleep and awake.

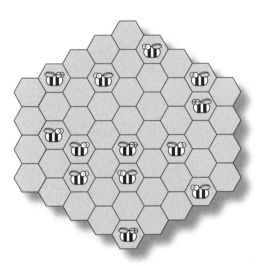

SMART BRAIN ACTION

A strategy used by teachers of creative thinking is to ask "What would X do?" Ask yourself a question such as, "What would St. Francis of Assisi do if a neighbor stole leeks from his vegetable garden?" You can change person and situation as you wish.

STAY SMART PUZZLE 44

TILE ALIGN

Place the eight tiles in the grid alongside the one tile provided so that all adjacent numbers match up where tiles align. Tiles may be rotated through 360 degrees, but none may be flipped over.

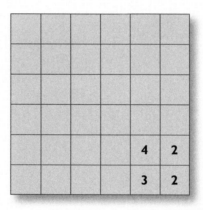

SMART BRAIN FACT

Learning a new skill, such as juggling, improves brain power. Oxford University scientists reported in 2009 that volunteers who learned to juggle for 6 weeks had a 5 percent increase in "white matter" (see page 18).

STAY SMART PUZZLE 45
MISSING CENTER

Here's a second chance to try our Digital Hubs challenge, which you first encountered at Puzzle 16. As before, your task is to work out the missing number from the center of Hub B. To do this, study the relationships between the numbers in Hub A and apply them to Hub B.

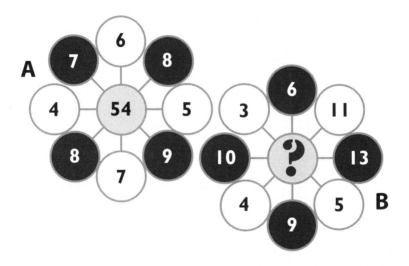

SMART BRAIN ACTION

Give your numerical intelligence a work-out with these simple percentage problems (try to do them in less than a minute if you can): What is 60 percent of 5? 40 percent of 20? 20 percent of 220?

STAY SMART PUZZLE 46
RAINBOW RICE

Try to memorize the list of words below. As we've seen, memory experts recommend processing information as much as possible to make it easier to recall. In this case, try to create visual images for the words in the list.

You'll notice that some of the words I've provided may be easier to visualize than others.

Commit the list to memory as well as you can, then cover the book, take a sheet of paper, and write the words down in the correct sequence.

In a couple of hours (or days), return to the list and try to learn it a second time. But now, make an extra effort to create visual images even for the more abstract words. If you can, link the images to your other senses as well—what can you hear? Is there a sensation associated with the image? Then do the test again. Do you notice any difference in your performance?

WORD LIST   Cat–glory–rainbow–table–literacy–pacifism–laptop–apple–baby–doubt–toast–sequence–church–Francophile–tractor–traveler–rice

SMART BRAIN FACT

In a celebrated test at University College, London, the city's registered black cab drivers were found to have an enlarged hippocampus (a brain region associated with finding your way around and laying down new memories).

STAY SMART PUZZLE 47
PERFECT PATTERN

In order to complete this grid in a logical pattern, you have to work out which of the square designs in this puzzle should be used to fill places A, B, and C.

This puzzle revisits Take Your Place (Puzzle 29): As you'll remember, this requires an eye for detail and clear thinking to identify the perfect pattern in the layout.

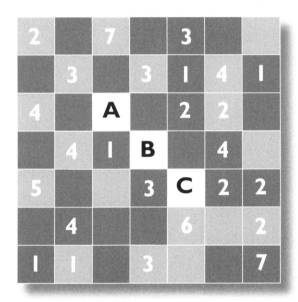

SMART BRAIN ACTION

Work on your visualization skills. Create a visual image for each letter of the alphabet, draw them on a sheet of paper or the Notes and Scribbles pages, then apply the images to memorize these words. For example: 1. Car 2. Apple 3. Tree. 4. Parrot.

STAY SMART PUZZLE 48
NO DOUBLES

This is a fresh chance to work at the Numberfit game we introduced at Puzzle 27. As before, you have to place the numbers 1–9 in each row. Numbers may appear multiple times in columns.

The puzzle is called No Doubles because identical numbers may not appear in neighboring squares (even diagonally). Some diagonal totals are provided around the outside of the grid.

Diagonal totals (top): 16 24   17 12

4		5			8	1		
7	8	4			2	6		
9		7	4	6	1	5		
6		3	8	2	5		7	
	6			1	4	5	9	
3	7	8			5	6		
5		2	3	8			1	
	6		1		3	4	7	
7				8			5	4

Left diagonal totals: 22, 18, 10
Right diagonal totals: 27, 10, 14

SMART BRAIN FACT

Older brains benefit from encountering the unexpected and the challenge of engaging with opposing ideas. Look for ways to introduce the unexpected into your routine. Change your newspaper or other source of news; try a new genre of movies or music.

STAY SMART PUZZLE 49
ALL IN ONE PLACE

This is an intriguing fitment puzzle. The rules are these: Each row and column should contain the numbers 1–7. The numbers placed in a heavily outlined set of squares must produce the calculation in the top-left corner, using the mathematical symbol provided, in any order. Any block of one square will contain the number in the top-left corner. For instance, in the example shown below, the numbers 4, 3, and 3 total 36 when multiplied.

SMART BRAIN ACTION

Can you recall the last three times you've come across the number of your age? Say you're 67... where have you recently seen 67? In someone's date of birth, on a bus, or on a price tag, perhaps? Can you remember anything significant that happened in 1967?

ONE TO NINE

Try your hand again at our grid navigation challenge (see Puzzle 12). As before, you must place the digits 1–9 in the grid so that it is possible to jump from one digit to the next, in order, using the steps provided. Each step must be used once. Both parts of a step must be used but can be taken in any order. No part of a step can pass over a dark square.

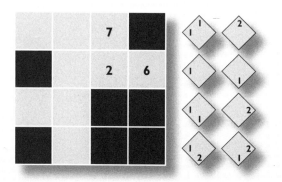

SMART BRAIN FACT

Running two days a week promotes the growth of new cells in brain areas connected to creating and recalling memories, according to research by Cambridge University and the U.S. National Institute on Aging, Maryland.

STAY SMART PUZZLE 51
TEN TO REMEMBER

Choose a scene: Go to your nearest park, or a piece of local countryside you love; alternatively, take in the view from your study, bedroom, or living room. Study the scene for 90 seconds and pay conscious attention to ten things you don't normally notice.

Note the ten things down on a scrap of paper. Next, take a break for 10 minutes. Then take another sheet of paper and write down as many of the ten things as you can.

Try again after an hour—look back at the original list to remind yourself of any sights you have forgotten. It might help at this stage to close your eyes and visualize them again, one by one. Then try again after 2 hours.

SMART BRAIN ACTION

Boost your number confidence with this sum. Answer it, then devise three steps (a multiplication, a division, and an addition or subtraction) to return from the answer to the starting point. $3 + 5 - 6 + 34 \div 9 \times 13 + 48 - 3 + 117 = $ **?**

STAY SMART PUZZLE 52
SHAPE ALIGN

Keep working on your concentration and memory with this shape and letter puzzle, a chance to apply what you picked up when doing Puzzle 14.

As before, your task is to fill up the box so that each row, column, and long diagonal contains four different shapes and all the letters A, B, C, and D.

SMART BRAIN FACT

To protect your brain health, keep an eye on your vitamin B12 intake. A 2010 study at the Karolinska Institute in Stockholm of people aged 65–79 found that those with low B12 levels seemed more likely to develop Alzheimer's.

TOU WETS—WIHT HET WOCYOBS

This anagram puzzle is really called "Out West—with the Cowboys." A group of great Hollywood cowboy actors has ridden off into the sunset under assumed identities—can you work out who's who on the range?

Tip: They're all very famous Hollywood stars! And they're all cowboys …

NAMES
1 Nohj Wenya
2 Fejf Gebrids
3 Tongemmory Tlicf
4 Semaj Tewstar
5 Tlinc Stoowead
6 Renhy Dafon
7 Nekiv Nostrec

Language puzzles like this boost your alertness and speed of thought, both of which are key to good memory performance.

SMART BRAIN ACTION

Here's a thirty-second test designed to get all your cylinders firing under pressure!
Find the answer to this sum:
$1 + 2 + 3 + 4 + 5 + 6 + 7 + 8 + 9 + 10 - 9 - 8 - 7 - 6 - 5 - 4$?

STAY SMART PUZZLE 54
PARTITION PLAN

Draw in the walls in the restaurant space below to partition it into separate seating areas (some walls are already drawn in for you). Each area must contain two circles (tables), the area sizes must match those shown below, and each + must be linked to at least two walls.

This puzzle tests and develops your visualization skills.

AREA SIZES   2, 3, 4, 4, 6, 6

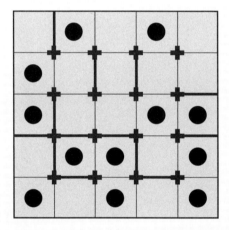

SMART BRAIN FACT

Meditating appears to improve the memory. Research at the University of California, L.A., in 2010 showed that, compared to others, regular meditators had a larger hippocampus (a brain area key to learning and memory).

STAY SMART PUZZLE 55
SAFECRACKER

Are you a safecracker? All twenty buttons must be pressed in the correct order, finishing with the "Open" button. The order is indicated by the numbers and directions on the buttons. Use your logic and working memory to make your way backward from the open button and determine which is the first button in the sequence.

SMART BRAIN ACTION

Complete these sums. Each y represents a mathematical symbol (× ÷ − +) and each symbol is used once in each sum:

55 y 2 y 30 y 4 y 8 = 17   13 y 6 y 4 y 19 y 1 = 3

STAY SMART PUZZLE 56
MARINE MANEUVERS

Develop your tactical thinking and visual logic with our version of the Battleships game.

Your task is to place the six listed ships into the diagram. A number and an arrow pointing to a line of hexagonal shapes refers to the number of shapes in that direction that are occupied by part of one or more ships. A ship may run in any direction, but no part of one ship touches any part of another. Begin by putting a small cross in those hexagons that you know to be empty, then shade in those you know to be occupied by part of a ship.

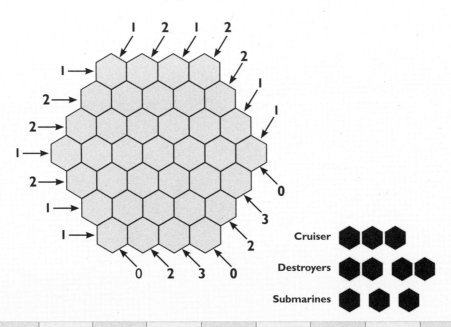

SMART BRAIN FACT

Are you musical? Practicing and performing music preserves the memory and protects your ability to hear clearly against background noise, according to 2011 research conducted at Northwestern University, Chicago.

STAY SMART PUZZLE 57
CARDS ON THE TABLE

Can you deduce the face value and suit of each of the cards below from these clues? Together they total 87. All twelve cards are of different values. In the pack, the values of the cards are as per their numbers, and Ace = 1, Jack = 11, Queen = 12, and King = 13. No card is horizontally or vertically next to another of the same color (hearts and diamonds are red; spades and clubs are black) and there are four different suits in every horizontal row and three different suits in each vertical column.

1 The two is of a different suit from that of the Queen, which is directly below the six, which is directly below the five.

2 The three is directly next to and right of the King, which is directly next to and above the eight of hearts.

3 Card H is of a different suit from that of card I, which has a value two lower than that of card H. Card E (which isn't a club) has a value one lower than that of card C.

4 The nine is of the same suit as the seven, which is in a lower row than the nine.

SMART BRAIN ACTION

Can you fix these ten British sea areas in your memory: Viking; North Utsire; South Utsire; Forties; Cromarty; Forth; Tyne; Dogger; Fisher; German Bight? Try making up a melody to sing them to to see if it helps.

STAY SMART PUZZLE 58

NUMBER STEPS

Do you work accurately under time pressure? Starting at the top left, work as fast as you can down from one box to another, applying the mathematical instructions to your running total.

There are three time limits, according to level—easy: 90 seconds; medium: 60 seconds; tough: 45 seconds.

Speed is of the essence: Use the stopwatch on your digital watch or smartphone to time yourself. But keep well away from the calculator function—this puzzle is strictly mental arithmetic only!

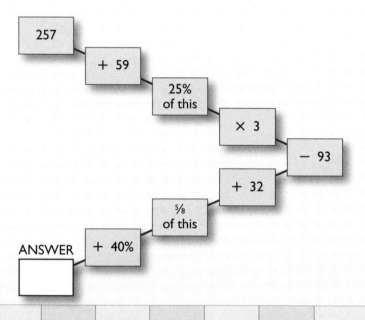

257

+ 59

25% of this

× 3

− 93

+ 32

⅝ of this

ANSWER   + 40%

SMART BRAIN FACT

Engaging your emotions can help memory performance (see page 34). But failing to manage them can interfere with thinking. If you are afraid of failing or fuming with anger then you'll struggle to learn or recall facts effectively.

STAY SMART PUZZLE 59
CUBE CUTE

This is another chance to demonstrate your facility in visualizing 3-D shapes (see Puzzle 30). Which two of these block piles could be fitted neatly together to make a perfect cube?

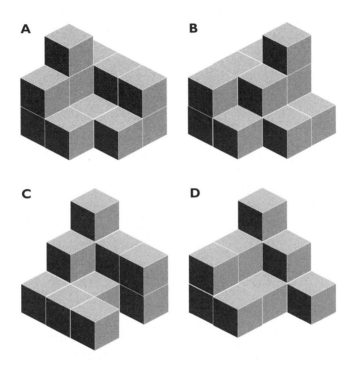

A   B

C   D

SMART BRAIN ACTION

Time to think logically. Try to deduce what the missing numbers are in this number sequence:

126 9 347 14 222 ? 541 ? 476 17 211 4 555 ? 219 12 743 ? 327 12

STAY SMART PUZZLE 60

CASINO TRIAL

Test your ability to juggle numbers under pressure: Imagine you're a high-roller on holiday in Las Vegas and this is a new gambling game. Can you use the totals given to calculate the price for the items in the largest box?

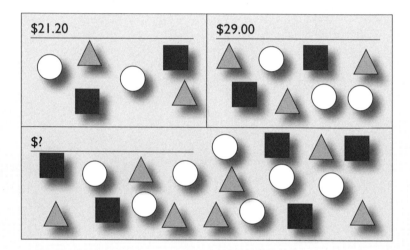

SMART BRAIN FACT

Caffeine may be able to reverse memory loss associated with Alzheimer's disease, according to 2009 research at the University of South Florida. Researchers then set out to find out if dementia sufferers might benefit from drinking coffee and taking supplements.

STAY SMART PUZZLE 61
THE (UN)USUAL SUSPECTS

This recognition exercise is a good way to test (and develop) your eye for detail and short-term memory. You have to study this grid of faces for 1 minute, then cover them up to answer the questions below. Imagine yourself at a line-up in a police station: Aren't the suspects maddeningly similar?

1   How many characters have both a beard and a hat?
2   Are there more gray hats or dark purple hats?
3   How many characters have sunglasses but no beard?
4   How many characters are hatless?
5   How many beards are there in the middle row?
6   Are there more sunglasses or regular glasses?
7   Are there any characters with neither a hat nor a beard?
8   In which row is the beardless character in the white hat?
9   What color hat is between two dark purple beret wearers?
10 Does the guy with the star on his hat have a beard?

SMART BRAIN ACTION

Think of ten heroes or heroines. Can you visualize each as a cookie or cake (flapjacks/donuts/croissants/cupcakes etc.)? Run through the sequence of people to recall all the treats/items on the list.

STAY SMART PUZZLE 62

NUMBER PILE

This is a second appearance for our pyramid add-up challenge (see Puzzle 20). As before, the puzzle is to be done as quickly as you can and the design is simple: In each pyramid, the number in each circle is the sum of the two numbers in the circles underneath it; your task is to fill in the empty circles to complete the pyramids.

As an additional challenge, imagine a number pyramid in which the four baseline numbers are your birthday in the format xx/xx month/date, and complete it to the top.

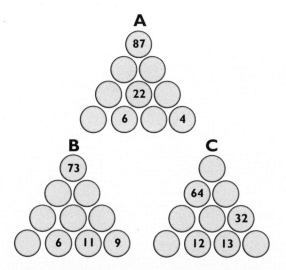

SMART BRAIN FACT

Brain surgery can be performed on fully conscious patients: The brain itself has no pain receptors. A brain surgery patient needs only local anesthetic to eliminate the pain of making incisions in the skull.

STAY SMART PUZZLE 63
A WHISK THROUGH SOME WHISKIES

Study this list of nine single-malt Scotch whiskies for 2 minutes, then close the book and write down the list in order. Try to get the (sometimes less than straightforward) spellings completely right.

To aid recall, use one or more of the memory techniques from the list below. There are two approaches—either lucky dip or combine accumulator.

For the lucky dip, before you look at the list, choose a number between 1 and 5, then use the corresponding technique from the list. For the combine accumulator, use as many of the five techniques as you can manage.

THE WHISKIES
Auchentoshan • Balvenie • Dufftown • Glenburgie • Glendronach
Glentauchers • Miltonduff • Strathisla • Tomintoul

Strategy 1: Try converting the initial letters of each into a number
(A = 1, B = 2, etc.)

Strategy 2: Create a character (or choose a celebrity or fictional hero/
heroine) for each.

Strategy 3: Make up a song featuring the names of the whiskies.

Strategy 4: Create a mnemonic featuring the names of the whiskies.

Strategy 5: Identify each with a place in a house or some outdoor area you
know well, then imagine a walk incorporating all of the places.

SMART BRAIN ACTION

This 30-second challenge develops the working memory. Study these artists' birthplaces and dates then try to write them down exactly as they are here. Renoir (Limoges, 1841), Rembrandt (Leiden, 1606), Raphael (Urbino, 1483), Rubens (Siegen, 1577).

STAY SMART PUZZLE 64

LETTER JACKS

The children's game of jacks inspired this challenge. In the game children grab many-pointed jacks in the time it takes a rubber ball to bounce. In this puzzle the letters on each "jack" are valued 1–26 according to their places in the alphabet. Your task is to crack the mystery code to reveal the missing letter.

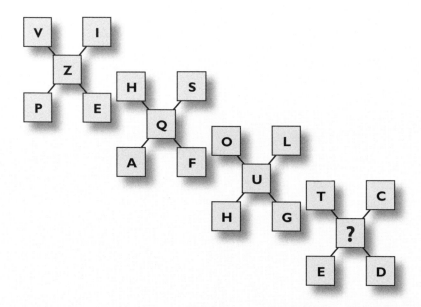

SMART BRAIN FACT

The benefits of learning new skills apply particularly strongly when it comes to languages. One program in Toronto, Canada, showed that bilingual people with Alzheimer's suffered significantly less mental decline than fellow sufferers who spoke just one language.

STAY SMART PUZZLE 65
ART BLOCKS

The Art Blocks challenge consists of seven columns of lettered balls: Remove a ball and the others above it will drop down in its place. Your task is to remove one ball from each column so that when all of the other balls drop down, they will spell out the names of six famous painters reading across (the artist at the top can already be seen). What are they, and which seventh artist will be spelled out by the seven balls you remove?

SMART BRAIN ACTION

Try our "+ × −" sums. Simply perform the mathematical operations in sequence.
A: $1 + 2 \times 3 − 4 + 5 \times 6 − 7 + 9$ and
B: $5 + 4 \times 3 − 2 + 1 \times 2 − 3 + 4 \times 5 − 6 + 7 \times 8 − 9$.

SOUNDS LIKE ...

Here's another technique for learning and recalling numbers, similar to the one outlined at Puzzle 26. While previously you created a visual image to match a number's shape, this time you create an image to match its sound: 4 could be an oar; 5 an Olympic swimmer making a dive; 9 a pine (tree) ... and so on.

Come up with your images for 0–9 then use them to memorize the numbers shown below. It's an important part of the process to draw the images you choose, either on this page, the Notes and Scribbles pages, or on a separate sheet of paper.

4,025
7,963

SMART BRAIN FACT

Scientists have measured different brainwave patterns associated with particular states of mind such as beta brainwaves (14–40 cycles per second) when alert or alpha brainwaves (9–14) when resting.

CHALLENGING MEMORY JOGGERS

The narrator of Saul Bellow's novella THE BELLAROSA CONNECTION, a memory expert, declares, "Memory is life." Well, with the memory function as in other areas of life, we improve with practice: You should find that as you return to particular puzzle types your performance is better, and that as you exercise your memory you hone your powers of recall. It's now time to attempt our most challenging puzzles and exercises ...

STAY SMART PUZZLE 67

LETTER LANDSCAPE

Here's your second chance to attempt our Navigator challenge (see Puzzle 33). As before, every oval shape in the diagram contains a different letter of the alphabet from A–K inclusive. Use the clues to determine their locations.

1 The C is due south of the H, which is next to and west of the B.
2 The G is next to and north of the I. The I is farther west than the E and farther north than the A.
3 The K is farther south than the F, but farther north than the H.
4 The J (which is due north of the D) is next to and east of the F.

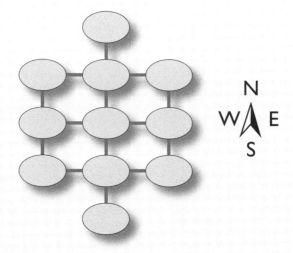

SMART BRAIN FACT

The brain may look fairly firm and rubbery, but it's actually quite soft, like jelly. Some people liken its consistency to that of warm butter. The reason it's so soft is that it contains a lot of fat: In fact, around 60 percent of your brain consists of fats.

DOMINOLOGICAL

Lay out a set of dominoes in four rows. The numbers indicate the values shown on all the dominoes in each column and the relevant half of the domino in every row. Work out where each domino is placed by comparing rows and columns to determine the possible positions of certain dominoes: For instance, if any column contains only one 6, then the domino 6/6 isn't in that column.

A set of dominoes consists of:
0/0, 0/1, 0/2, 0/3, 0/4, 0/5, 0/6, 1/1, 1/2, 1/3, 1/4, 1/5, 1/6, 2/2, 2/3, 2/4, 2/5, 2/6, 3/3, 3/4, 3/5, 3/6, 4/4, 4/5, 4/6, 5/5, 5/6, 6/6.

	0, 1, 1, 2, 2, 2, 3, 6	0, 1, 1, 1, 3, 2, 4, 6	0, 0, 3, 3, 3, 4, 4, 6	0, 0, 0, 2, 3, 5, 5, 6	1, 2, 2, 2, 3, 3, 6, 6	0, 4, 4, 5, 5, 5, 5, 6	1, 1, 4, 4, 4, 5, 5, 6
0, 0, 2, 4, 4, 6, 6							
2, 3, 3, 5, 6, 6, 6							
0, 1, 3, 3, 4, 5, 6							
2, 3, 3, 4, 5, 5, 5							
0, 0, 2, 2, 4, 5, 5							
1, 1, 2, 2, 3, 5, 6							
0, 0, 1, 1, 1, 4, 6							
0, 1, 1, 2, 3, 4, 4							

SMART BRAIN ACTION

Can you spot the odd one out in the following list of locations?
Argentina; Peru; Austria; Colombia; Mexico City; Italy; Venezuela; Guyana; Mozambique; Paraguay; Vatican City.

STAY SMART PUZZLE 69
DO DOTTY

This is a second chance to excel at the Dice Path puzzle we introduced on page 46 (Puzzle 34). As before, each shade represents a direction (up, down, left, or right) and the number of dots on each die tells you how far to go. If you start in the top-left die of the maze and follow the directions correctly, you will visit every die in turn once only. Can you work out which shade represents which direction and determine which die is the last you visit on your trip?

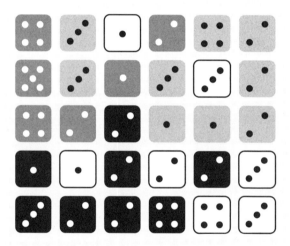

SMART BRAIN FACT

If you drink beetroot juice you boost blood flow to your brain, improving brain performance including the memory, according to a 2010 study at Wake Forest University in Winston-Salem, North Carolina.

STAY SMART PUZZLE 70

GONE TO THE COGS

Here is a third chance to try this engaging challenge (see Puzzles 6 and 37), although this time with a fourth cog wheel added. Revisiting puzzle types is a good way to measure your improvement.

In this version, cog A has seven teeth, cog B eight, cog C fourteen, and cog D twelve; your task is to determine how many revolutions cog A must be turned to bring all three cogs back to their starting positions.

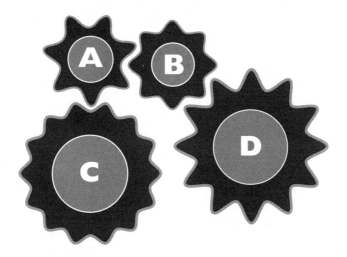

SMART BRAIN ACTION

First, sort out this jumbled list of celebrated composers. Then close the book and try to remember them. Byrd Ludwig van Offenbach Edward Britten Wolfgang Monteverdi Amadeus Beethoven Elgar William Benjamin Claudio Jacques Mozart.

STAY SMART PUZZLE 71
ELIMINATOR

In this Number Eliminator puzzle, your task is to shade in squares so that no number occurs more than once in any row or column. Shaded squares cannot touch one another either horizontally or vertically (although they may touch diagonally at a corner), and all unshaded squares must form a single continuous area.

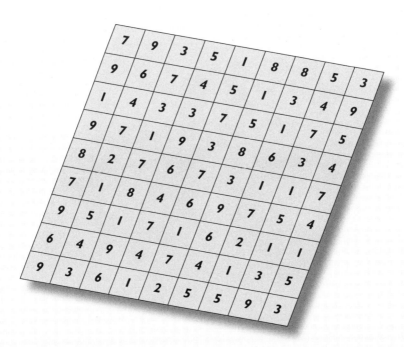

SMART BRAIN FACT

Reciting poems or favorite passages from books out loud and writing and redrafting letters or documents have been shown to improve memory function as well as overall mental performance. Doing mental arithmetic brings the same benefits.

STAY SMART PUZZLE 72
PICTURE PERFECT

A key memory strategy—as we have seen—is to connect verbal information to your other senses. You tried learning while inhaling a scent, and while savoring a distinctive taste (page 30); and you experimented with creating visual prompts to correspond to numbers' shapes or sounds (pages 37 and 78) or funny pictures to make names memorable (page 54). Another aspect of this tried and tested technique is to make a large drawing while inputting information to your memory. Use as much color and memorable detail as you can. Include rude or funny elements, caricatures of people you know, and so on.

For this exercise try making a drawing to commit this list of Canadian provinces and territories to memory:

PLACE NAMES Ontario; Quebec; Nova Scotia; New Brunswick; Manitoba; British Columbia; Prince Edward Island; Saskatchewan; Alberta; Newfoundland and Labrador; Northwest Territories; Yukon; Nunavut

After you've finished the picture put it aside; come back to this puzzle after around 30 minutes and try to write out the full list. Try again after an hour, then after half a day or so.

SMART BRAIN ACTION

Add the digits in the birth dates of actors Michael Caine (03/14/1933) and Bob Hoskins (10/26/1942), then divide by 7. Add the answer to the sum of the birth dates of directors Mike Leigh (02/20/1943) and Ken Loach (06/17/1936). What's the answer?

STAY SMART PUZZLE 73

BOYS IN BLUE

This is a reprise of our logic puzzle Downtown Parking (see Puzzle 18).
However, this time the three darker cars entering the district are not Mafia
limousines but unmarked police cars tailing the original vehicles. As before,
there are three cars and three sets of directions: Each set of directions will
take one car to a garage, but which car to which garage?

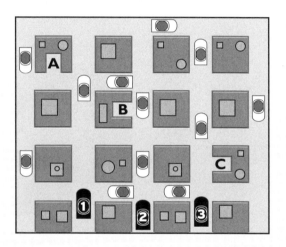

DIRECTIONS **i** Take the third turning on the left, then second left, first left then
second right, and turn left.

ii Take the first right, then first left, then first left, second right, first
left, and turn right.

iii Take the third right, then second right, first right, first right again,
and turn left.

SMART BRAIN FACT

How do we remember a face? A 2009 study at the University of Barcelona found that we
don't take in faces all at once—we look first at a person's eyes, second at the mouth, third
at the nose. Being conscious of this can help you commit someone's face to memory.

STAY SMART PUZZLE 74

CUBE-A-CUBA

Think back to how you solved Puzzles 30 and 59 as we take a third pass at this brick challenge, an excellent way of developing your confidence at manipulating shapes in three dimensions. This time the final shape is larger, and your task is to work out which two of the block piles A–D would fit together to make a 4x4x4 cube.

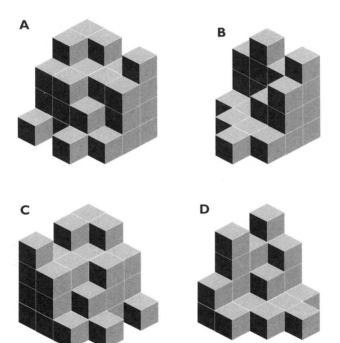

A

B

C

D

SMART BRAIN ACTION

Read this list of 13 typical office items, then close the book and try to recall them in the correct order: keyboard; telephone; printer; file; mousemat; monitor; adhesive tape; mouse; glue; pen; memory stick; scissors; hole punch.

STAY SMART PUZZLE 75

NUMBER CRUNCH

Fill the grid with numbers 1–6 so that each number appears once in every row and column. The clues refer to the digit totals in the squares—for example: A 1 2 3 + 6 means that the numbers in squares A1, A2, and A3 add up to 6. A B 1 + 5 means that the numbers in squares A1 and B1 add up to 5.

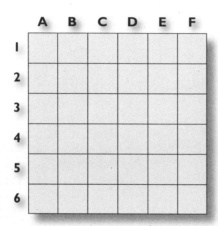

1 A 5 6 + 5

2 A B 1 + 5

3 A B 4 + 3

4 A B C 2 + 13

5 B C 5 + 9

6 B C 6 + 8

7 C 3 4 + 10

8 C D 4 + 10

9 D 4 5 + 8

10 D E 3 + 4

11 E 1 2 + 10

12 F 4 5 6 + 14

SMART BRAIN FACT

Naps can really enhance your brain performance. A 2009 research study at the University of California found that people who had a 60-minute nap after lunch significantly improved their capacity to learn and recall new facts.

DIVIDE BY RULE

Let's revisit our Shikaku spatial challenge (see Puzzles 21 and 39). As before, your task is to draw rules to divide the grid into rectangles, each of which contains a single digit indicating the number of boxes in the rectangle.

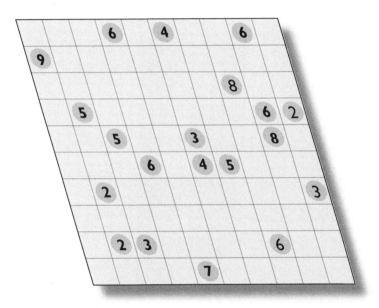

SMART BRAIN ACTION

Try using jatapatha again (page 22) to learn the names of the first eight U.S. presidents: George Washington, John Adams, Thomas Jefferson, James Madison, James Monroe, John Quincy Adams, Andrew Jackson, Martin Van Buren.

STAY SMART PUZZLE 77

ARE YOU PAYING ATTENTION?

Time to work on your short- and longer-term memory: This quiz tests your recollection of what's happened to you—both recently and over the years. We focus on a mix of memorable and minor events.

Don't think too hard: Try to answer all the questions inside 2 minutes.

1 What color were the seats in the first car you ever owned? ....

2 How many different fruits did you eat yesterday? ....

3 What was the street address of the first house you lived in? ....

4 What was the last travel ticket you bought? ....

5 Can you remember your earliest telephone number? ....

6 What was the first name of your best friend's father when you were ten years old? ....

7 Think back to last year. What was the last novel or non-fiction book that you read? ....

8 What is/was the first name of your mother's father? ....

9 What color socks/underwear did you wear yesterday? ....

10 What was the weather like last Wednesday? ....

SMART BRAIN FACT

Research at the University of Bristol in 2011 identified three brain areas—the hippocampus, perihinal cortex, and medial prefrontal cortex—that work together in a memory circuit if we need to recall where we left something, such as a book or spectacles.

ARE YOU PAYING ATTENTION?

11 When was the last time you read a newspaper different from the one you habitually buy? Which paper was it? ....

12 Think back two days. What did you have for lunch on that day? ....
....

13 Who was the first person you spoke to yesterday on the telephone—and on your cellphone? ....

14 Aside from furniture, name the largest thing in your house/apartment. ....
....

15 Think back to the first car you can remember your parents owning. What color was it? ....

16 What was the most expensive thing you purchased yesterday? ....

17 What was the name of the first hotel you stayed in? ....

18 What was the last but one airline you used? ....

19 What was the last meal you cooked or ate containing rice? ....

20 What was the first piece of furniture you bought? ....

SMART BRAIN ACTION

Try to complete this quickfire brain-jogger activity in less than a minute. If Picasso is KRXZHHL and Van Gogh is EZM TLTS, who are TZFTFRM, NRXSVOZMTVOL, and NLMVG?

STAY SMART PUZZLE 78

DOMINO MAP

Can you lay out a standard set of twenty-eight dominoes so they match the numbers in the grid? The check-box is provided as an aid, while one domino has been put in place to get you started.

0–0	0–1	0–2	0–3	0–4	0–5	0–6	1–1	1–2	1–3	1–4	1–5	1–6	2–2
												✔	

2–3	2–4	2–5	2–6	3–3	3–4	3–5	3–6	4–4	4–5	4–6	5–5	5–6	6–6

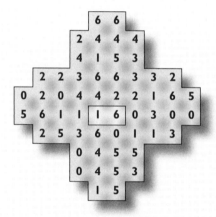

SMART BRAIN FACT

Being mentally active and taking physical exercise are the two most important preventive measures you can take against mental decline and developing Alzheimer's disease, according to 2011 research.

STAY SMART PUZZLE 79
LOST LEADER

Fancy yourself as a codebreaker? This code sudoku puzzle, which comes in three parts, will test you out.

First, complete the two grids so that every row and column contains the letters BCFMXZ in the first, and the numbers 123456 in the second.

Second, decode the finished grids—add the numbers in the shaded squares to the letters in the matching shaded squares (so, A + 3 = D, Y + 4 = C, etc.) to get six new letters.

Finally, rearrange your new letters to spell the name of a politically and socially influential figure from the last century.

M			C		
	M		Z		B
				B	
		X	F		M
B		F			X
				X	F

	2			1	
6				1	
	4	3	6		
					5
	1	2		6	
5				4	3

SMART BRAIN ACTION

Are you familiar with the Seven Deadly Sins? Study the list for 30 seconds, then close the book and write them down. Lust; Gluttony; Avarice; Sloth; Wrath; Envy; Pride. Can you come up with a good mnemonic to help you remember them?

STAY SMART PUZZLE 80
FINETUNING YOUR MEMORY

Music helps you remember. If you listen to a particular piece of music when learning, playing the same music back will boost your powers of recall. Why not try it?

Take two articles (from a newspaper, magazine, or journal). Read one in silence and one while listening to your chosen piece of music. Take a break for an hour or two then try to recall the facts. For the first article recall in silence, for the second play the same music a second time. Notice any difference in your memory performance?

Or try singing. Take this list of some of the world's great rivers. Try learning it as a singsong for 2 minutes.

RIVERS   Euphrates, Missouri, Murray, Thames, Yellow, Tyne, Rio Grande, Niger, Yukon, Danube, Mississippi, Indus, Nile, Ohio, Amazon, Yangtze, Volga

Close the book and see if you can write the list out in sequence.

SMART BRAIN FACT

Long-term stress has a negative effect on memory. Try meditation to help you manage the effects. Or juice. A 2011 study at Queen Margaret University, Edinburgh, found that drinking pomegranate juice each day reduced levels of the stress hormone cortisol.

STAY SMART PUZZLE 81
EIGHT SQUARE

Work on your focus, numerical confidence, and clarity of thinking with this Eight Square puzzle. Your task is to fill in the grid so that every horizontal row and vertical column of eight circles contains the numbers 1–8 inclusive. The white circles contain the odd numbers 1, 3, 5, and 7, while the shaded circles contain the even numbers 2, 4, 6, and 8. Some numbers are already in place to get you started.

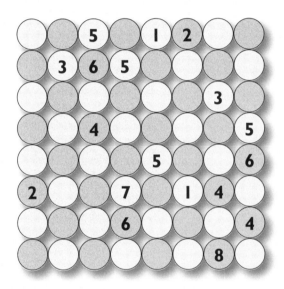

SMART BRAIN ACTION

Imagine that in August 1980, George Cukor (born 07/07/1899) looks back at his movies *The Philadelphia Story*, *A Star is Born*, and *My Fair Lady*, adds the digits in their years of release (1940, 1954, 1964) and subtracts the total from his age. What's the answer?

MAGIC CARPET

Here's a variation on the "memory walk" we used on page 26 (Puzzle 15). This time you're taking a ride on a magic flying carpet. As you look down, imagine the scenes you will see round about you and use them to fix the following modes of transport in your memory . Make sure you learn them in the correct sequence.

Afterward, cover the book, take a sheet of paper or turn to the Notes and Scribbles pages, and attempt to write down the list in sequence.

Imagine reliving the magic carpet ride and seeing the series of images below in order to boost your powers of recall.

LIST OF ITEMS Bicycle—Tractor—Horsedrawn coach—Taxicab—Tandem—
Van—Unicycle—Double-decker bus—Airliner—Truck—
Executive jet—Baby's buggy—Hang-glider—Sled—Train

SMART BRAIN FACT

A University of Cincinnati study reported in 2010 that a pint of blueberry juice a day combats memory loss caused by dementia. Another study found that purple grape juice had the same effect.

STAY SMART PUZZLE 83
CROSS SUM

Using the numbers below, complete these six equations (three reading across and three reading downward). Every number is used once and one is already in place.

THE NUMBERS 1 2 3 5 6 7 8 9

	+		×		=	45
−		+		−		
4	×		−		=	33
×		×		+		
	−		+		=	11
=		=		=		
24		20		9		

SMART BRAIN ACTION

You have 1 minute to rearrange these fruits in alphabetical order, then fix them in your memory. Afterward, close the book and list them all. Tomato, mango, banana, satsuma, grape, apple, loganberry, pomegranate, cherry, raspberry.

PUZZLE 84

WORD SUMS

Can you get your head around these brain-twisting word sums? They will exercise both the numerical and the language centers in your brain. And as I've noted earlier in the book, working your brain in this way will boost its performance and improve your working memory.

WORD SUMS
1 Months in a decade ÷ days in April.
2 Consonants in Mississippi + vowels in Missouri.
3 Letters in Antarctica − number of continents.
4 Minutes in a non-leap year − seconds in a day.
5 Oars used in a rowing eight + players in a soccer team.
6 Moons of Neptune x planets in solar system.
7 Letters in "Internet search engine" x consonants in "online security."

SMART BRAIN FACT

Neurogenesis—the creation of new cells in your brain —happens most of all in the first three years of your life. There is a second burst of brain-cell formation in puberty and a third when you are a young adult.

STAY SMART PUZZLE 85

INNER-CITY PILE-UP

Place the numbers 1–6 into each row and column. Each number represents a skyscraper of that many floors. Organize the skyscrapers in such a way that the given number outside the grid represents the number of buildings that can be seen from that point, looking only at that number's row or column. A skyscraper with a lower number of floors cannot hide a higher building, but one with a higher number of floors always hides any building behind it.

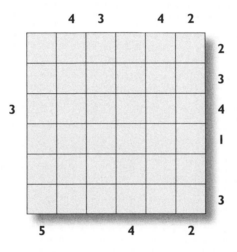

SMART BRAIN ACTION

Pin up a list of thirty-one facts you'd like to have at your fingertips. Put it somewhere you will see it each morning. Learn one a day and test yourself once a week. You could also do this with science or math formulae, spellings, or pronunciations of words.

STAY SMART PUZZLE 86

CARD SHARP

How sharp's your eye for cards? This memory test could be part of a mental training program ahead of a trip to the casinos of Las Vegas.

Take a pack of cards and select the spades and clubs: Lay these twenty-six cards face down on the table. Now turn over a card; look at the number (or picture) and suit, commit it to memory, then turn it back over. Repeat a total of ten times. Finally take a sheet of paper (or turn to the Notes and Scribbles pages at the back) and write down in order the ten cards, noting the suit and number/picture in each case.

TIP The exercise works better if you ask a friend to keep track as you go, so you can check your performance.

SMART BRAIN FACT

Research at Helsinki University in 2008 showed that stroke victims who listened to music for 2 hours a day recovered their memory and powers of attention better than others who listened to words or nothing at all.

STAY SMART PUZZLE 87
CODECRACKER

Here's a chance to try your hand again at our Letter Jacks challenge (see Puzzle 64). As before, the letters A–Z are valued 1–26 and your task is to crack the mystery code in order to identify the missing letter.

You use your working memory and hone your clarity of thinking in code challenges like this.

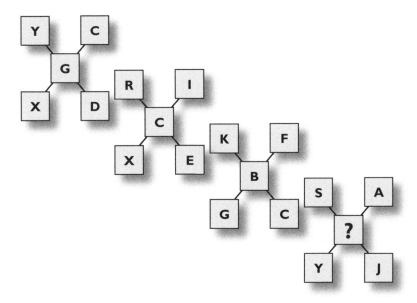

SMART BRAIN ACTION

Dream your way to a better memory. Some studies suggest that people who recall their dreams are more creative and motivated, which certainly benefits the memory. Tell yourself you'll remember your dreams before you go to sleep, and keep a pad and pencil handy.

STAY SMART PUZZLE 88
SEA WAR

Try our Battleships grid a second time (see Puzzle 56): Can you place the six listed ships into the diagram? As before, a number and arrow pointing to a line of hexagonal shapes refers to the number of shapes in that direction which are occupied by part of one or more ships; a ship may run in any direction, but no part of one ship touches any part of another. Begin by putting a small cross in those hexagons that you know to be empty, then shade in those that you know are occupied by part of a ship.

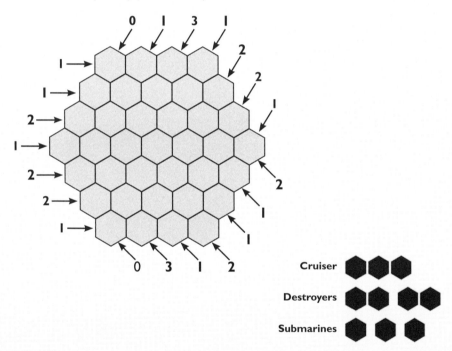

Cruiser

Destroyers

Submarines

SMART BRAIN FACT

Here's another reason to do puzzles and exercises that develop concentration. A 2005 study at the University of California, Berkeley, suggested that mental performance declines in older people because they find it harder to screen out distractions.

STAY SMART PUZZLE 89

NUMBERCOMB

Numbercomb provides an opportunity to put into practice any techniques or approaches you developed when working through Honeycomb Links (Puzzle 9). As before, some of the circles in the puzzle are already shaded. Fill in more white circles, so that the number of shaded circles totals the number inside the area they surround.

There is one rule: Every shaded circle surrounding an area with a number higher than "1" needs to be next to another shaded circle. When solving, it may help to put a small dot into any circle you know should not be filled.

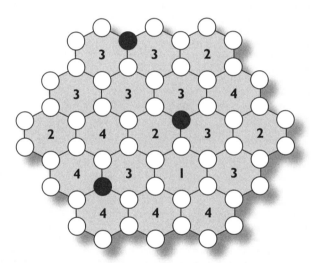

SMART BRAIN ACTION

The 14.10 train from London leaves 12 minutes late, falling 12 minutes further behind schedule at the first station, 11 at the second, 10 at the third, and so on. Refunds are given if the train is 70 minutes or more late at the sixth station. Will a refund be given?

STAY SMART PUZZLE 90
THREE MEN AND A BANK

You'll need full concentration to succeed at this close reading test. Read the story below twice only. Do not look at the questions on the right-hand page. Try hard to memorize the detail in the article. Now cover this page and attempt the questions without referring back to the story.

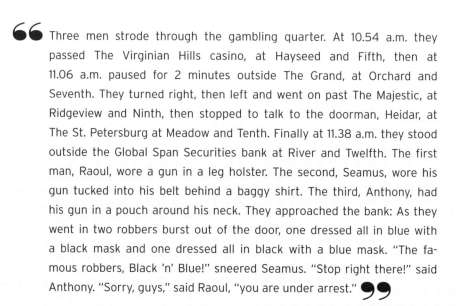

Three men strode through the gambling quarter. At 10.54 a.m. they passed The Virginian Hills casino, at Hayseed and Fifth, then at 11.06 a.m. paused for 2 minutes outside The Grand, at Orchard and Seventh. They turned right, then left and went on past The Majestic, at Ridgeview and Ninth, then stopped to talk to the doorman, Heidar, at The St. Petersburg at Meadow and Tenth. Finally at 11.38 a.m. they stood outside the Global Span Securities bank at River and Twelfth. The first man, Raoul, wore a gun in a leg holster. The second, Seamus, wore his gun tucked into his belt behind a baggy shirt. The third, Anthony, had his gun in a pouch around his neck. They approached the bank: As they went in two robbers burst out of the door, one dressed all in blue with a black mask and one dressed all in black with a blue mask. "The famous robbers, Black 'n' Blue!" sneered Seamus. "Stop right there!" said Anthony. "Sorry, guys," said Raoul, "you are under arrest."

SMART BRAIN FACT

The brain benefits from stimulation; having a conversation or a discussion are among the best ways to keep yourself alert and interested. A 2008 Harvard School of Public Health study found that an active social life may slow memory decline in older people.

THREE MEN AND A BANK

The memory questions—have you covered the page opposite?

1 What was the first casino the men passed? ....

2 At what time did they stop outside The Grand? ....

3 What is the address of the third casino? ....

4 What is the name of the doorman at the fourth casino? ....

5 What is the name of the bank? ....

6 What time do the men stand outside the bank? ....

7 What is the second man called? ....

8 How does the third man carry his gun? ....

9 How was the second bank robber dressed? ....

10 Who said, "Stop right there!"? ....

SMART BRAIN ACTION

Use visualization to memorize these directions. Straight on to Ray's Records, follow Fox Avenue as far as The Blue Bell Bar, right on Green Street past The Snip hair salon, left at The Apple Man greengrocers, go through the underpass, arrive at White's Pool Hall.

STAY SMART PUZZLE 91
BULL'S EYE

Which number should be in the center of Hub B? You're probably well practiced at this exercise after working through it at Puzzles 16 and 45.

As before, your task is to study the relationships between the numbers in Hub A and apply them to Hub B. Revisiting a puzzle enables you to reinforce the skills involved—just as when you're inputting facts to your memory, recapping what you have learned fixes the information in your memory.

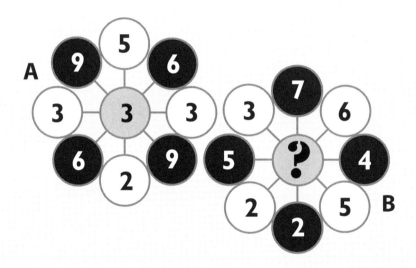

SMART BRAIN FACT

The brain consolidates memories and new information during sustained sleep, according to 2008 research at the University of Geneva. People taught a new skill performed better after 8 hours' sleep than those denied sleep or allowed only a nap.

SLOT IN

Cast your mind back to Puzzles 29 and 47. Here is another version of our grid-logic puzzle. Once again your task is to work out which of the square designs in this puzzle should be slotted in to fill places A, B, and C.

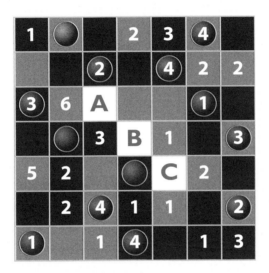

SMART BRAIN ACTION

Link the following colors to the fruits, then try to recall them all. (A color may apply to more than one fruit.) Greengage, yellow, raspberry, apple, purple, blueberry, green, kiwi fruit, orange, red, banana, plum, clementine, tomato, blue.

TOP TO BOTTOM

Can you find a way across this tiled floor, one tile at a time, starting and ending on the two dark tiles? You can tread only on squares with numbers divisible by seven or nine (or both) and you're not allowed to move diagonally, nor to jump over any tile.

■	99	51	16	7	14	54	70	21
40	63	54	35	39	91	92	26	72
21	92	33	81	75	84	80	36	98
7	99	98	49	67	35	38	18	31
45	30	20	22	24	99	94	35	18
91	14	77	90	42	9	68	97	27
35	34	70	73	23	76	81	63	77
36	96	51	93	27	54	28	26	14
41	84	7	21	42	32	97	65	74
42	28	25	37	29	84	36	70	56
66	81	49	63	90	56	69	95	■

SMART BRAIN FACT

Getting older seems to make us better able to stay positive. A 2006 Sydney University study using MRI scans showed that the brains of people aged 50–79 had more control over their responses to negative emotions than those of younger people.

STAY SMART PUZZLE 94

ONE STEP AT A TIME

You'll remember this task from Puzzles 13 and 41. You develop your facility with numbers by passing as quickly as you can down our twin number ladders. Start with the figure given, then follow the sums from top to bottom to reach two answers, one in each column.

EASY	TOUGH
7	**57**
Add 57	Multiply by 9
Divide by 4	Subtract 85
Add 61	Divide by 4
Divide by 11	Multiply by 6
Multiply by 9	Add 319
Subtract 13	Square root
Treble it	Add 444
Divide by 5	Divide by 19
Divide by 5	120% of it
ANSWER	ANSWER

SMART BRAIN ACTION

We've seen that emotional engagement aids memory performance (see page 34). Learn this sequence of colors by linking them to emotions such as joy, fear, or disgust. Purple, red, green, white, indigo, red, brown, yellow, purple.

STAY SMART PUZZLE 95
SPEEDY STEPS

Imagine you're discussing interest rates, house prices, or the pensions crisis—being confident with mental arithmetic can be a key aspect of appearing intelligent and well informed in everyday conversation; and it often feeds into and promotes good memory performance.

This puzzle—like its partner, Puzzle 58—requires you to follow a set of mathematical instructions accurately when working at speed. Starting at the top left, work as fast as you can down from one box to another, applying the mathematical instructions to your running total. There are three time limits, according to level—easy: 90 seconds; medium: 60 seconds; tough: 45 seconds.

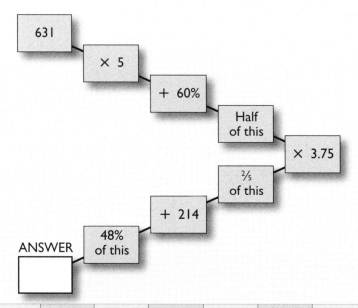

SMART BRAIN FACT

A University of Michigan project in 2010 found that people who carried on working well into their 60s performed better on memory tests than those who took early retirement in their 50s.

SHINING EXAMPLE

This illuminating puzzle provides a good test of logical-directional thinking; you may recognize the format from Puzzle 10, Lighten Up. As before, circles represent light bulbs. A bulb sends rays of light horizontally and vertically, illuminating its entire row and column unless its light is blocked by a dark cell. Your task is to place bulbs in empty squares so that no two bulbs shine on each other, until the entire grid is lit up.

Some dark cells contain numbers, indicating how many light bulbs are in squares either above, below, to the right, or to the left. Bulbs placed diagonally adjacent to a numbered cell do not contribute to the bulb count. An unnumbered dark cell may have any number of light bulbs adjacent to it, or none at all, and not all light bulbs are necessarily clued via dark squares.

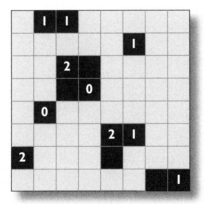

SMART BRAIN ACTION

You drive from London to Edinburgh (407 miles/655 km), then to Inverness (157 miles/252 km), then to Glasgow (171 miles/275 km), then to Preston (183 miles/295 km), and back to London (220 miles/354 km). How far is this?

STAY SMART PUZZLE 97

HEXAGON HOLD-UP

The numbers 0–9 fit perfectly in the hexagon grid, each appearing once in a white space and once in a dark space. Values of white hexagons must equal the sum of the values of the surrounding dark hexagons. If these values add up to a two-digit number, place the second digit in the white hexagon. For example: 4 + 5 + 3 = 12; place 2 in the hexagon.

This challenge, which you worked through before at Puzzle 25, Number Nest, makes a good mental warm-up.

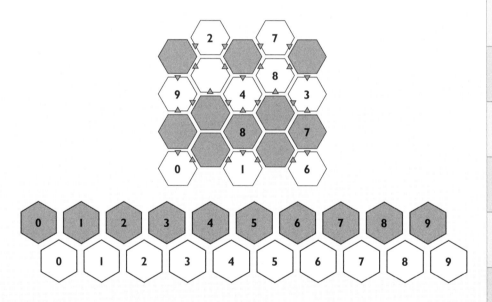

SMART BRAIN FACT

Research suggests we are changing the way we use our memory. Because we can look facts up very easily—for example, on the Internet—we focus less on remembering facts and more on remembering where to find them.

STAY SMART PUZZLE 98

NIGHTHAWKS

Test your powers of observation while enjoying some fine art. Find a reproduction of Edward Hopper's 1942 painting *Nighthawks*. (You can easily find one online—do an Internet search for "Hopper—*Nighthawks*.") Look at the picture for 2 minutes, taking note of as many details as possible, then look away and try to answer the following questions. No looking back at the picture! To make the most of your memory you need to be visually switched on and alert to detail.

1 How many people in the picture are not wearing hats?...

2 How many stools are visible and unoccupied?..

3 What is the name of the diner?..

4 How many urns are there?..

5 What color is the woman's dress? ....

6 How many windows are wholly visible in the upper story of the building opposite?...

7 What is behind the urns?..

8 Is the bartender leaning down or reaching up?...

9 Does the woman have short or long hair?..

SMART BRAIN ACTION

This number encodes the name of a celebrated twentieth-century artist. Can you crack the code and name him? 2, 15, 5, 26, 24, 2, 19, 9, 16, 13. Clue: This is a big shot—one of his paintings sold for 100 million U.S. dollars.

STAY SMART PUZZLE 99
PLATES IN THE NINTH POSITION

Imagine these are plates found on an antique stall: I'd like to arrange them in a logical layout, but I can't work out which one of the four alternatives A–D should occupy the ninth position.

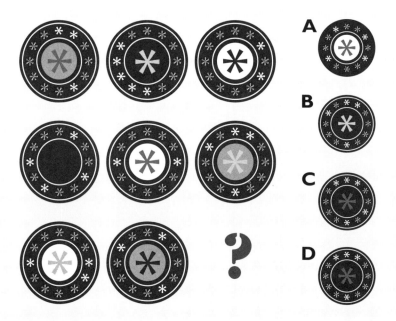

SMART BRAIN FACT

The hippocampus, the brain region we've encountered several times and know is closely involved in the formation of new memories, is in the limbic system, a part of the brain that governs appetites and urges.

STAY SMART PUZZLE 100
NUMBER CARD

To complete our final puzzle, Number Card, fill in the blank squares with whole numbers between 1 and 30 inclusive, any of which may occur more than once, or not at all. The numbers in every horizontal row add up to the totals on the right, as do the two long diagonal lines; while those in every vertical column add up to the totals along the bottom.

								154
13	6	2	15		25	4		**115**
24		19	8	26	13		10	**156**
	23	14	3		27	8	15	**115**
7		1		5		28	11	**94**
	13		6	16	1	20		**131**
3	29	12		10	21	9	6	**114**
4		28	9	23	17		21	**162**
18	15			5		17	22	**129**
98	**153**	**115**	**102**	**119**	**142**	**142**	**145**	**165**

SMART BRAIN ACTION

What do you get if you add the days in June, August, October, and December, then subtract the days in January, September, and April, add the days in May and November, and divide by the days in July?

THE ANSWERS

Try not to delve into the answer section too quickly. If you're stuck on a puzzle, take your time, perhaps go off and do something else for a while before you have another go. And when you do look at the solution, try to learn something new about the process used—this will help make sure you stay smart!

PUZZLE 1 The completed grid should look as shown below, matching all the octaclues—as in clue 4, for example, A (6) minus D (4) = H (2) or in clue 8, F (32) divided by H (2) = G (16).

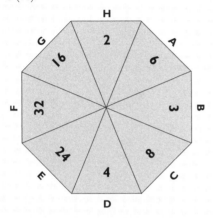

PUZZLE 2 The answers to our arithmetical work-out are shown below. For the Smart Brain Action, the images might be a sandy beach or an egg timer filled with sand (Sandy); an artist's easel or Art Garfunkel (Arturo); a giant ant or an image of Roman general Mark Antony or actor Anthony Quinn (Anthony).

A	**B**	**C**
5 + 3 = 8	9 + 4 = 13	11 − 8 = 3
6 + 5 = 11	4 × 7 = 28	21 ÷ 7 = 3
18 ÷ 3 = 6	32 − 23 = 9	31 + 6 =37
3 + 9 = 12	20 ÷ 5 = 4	44 ÷ 11 = 4
17 − 8 = 9	4 × 3 = 12	11 − 7 = 4
12 ÷ 3 = 4	3 + 5 = 8	5 − 3 = 2
22 − 7 = 15	8 ÷ 4 = 2	42 ÷ 7 = 6
9 × 7 = 63	12 × 5 = 60	13 × 3 = 39
29 − 13 = 16	13 − 8 = 5	11 + 6 = 17
7 × 8 = 56	14 + 13 = 27	21 + 11 = 32

PUZZLE 3 The continents are Europe, Antarctica, Asia, Africa, Australia, North America, South America. One popular mnemonic is Eat An Aspirin After A Nighttime Snack. The oceans are Indian, Atlantic, Arctic, Southern, Pacific. How about, "I am a special person" or "I ate a soft peach." For the added coastline challenge, how about "Can I guess Rachel's predilection?" or "Crying is good relaxation, probably."

PUZZLE 4 You should start in the shaded square 2S in the upper left: The grid is shown below. What you find in the box should bring the memories flooding in! Think back … what would you put in a childhood memory box?

N
↑

2S	1E	2W	2W	1S
2S	1S	1E	2W	2W
2E	2E		2N	2N
1E	1S	2E	1W	1N
2E	1W	2E	1N	1W

W ←   E →

↓
S

PUZZLE 5 The numbers represent the number of sides in the shape they occupy. When shapes overlap, the numbers are multiplied together.
A: 5 × 4 = 20 B: 10 × 4 × 4 = 160
B divided by A = 8.

PUZZLE 6 Seven revolutions of cog A, which will make exactly eight revolutions of cog B, and four revolutions of cog C. The problem develops your ability to visualize change. Maintaining or building self-confidence is an important aspect of keeping your memory strong; if you feel worried, the stress makes it more likely that you'll forget when you want to remember.

PUZZLE 7 If "red" is written in blue, the natural response is normally to say "red" rather than "blue" as required. To overcome this, you have to manage your attention: You override the first, instinctive response to make the one required by the rules of the test.

PUZZLE 8 Square B is the only one that replicates the pattern. The digital sequence is as follows: When reading from left to right, top to bottom, each number increases first by 2, then by 3, 4, 5, 6, 7, 8, and 9.

PUZZLE 9 The correct solution to the Honeycomb Links puzzle is as shown below. Each number matches the number of dark circles surrounding it. One aspect of the short-term memory (see Smart Brain Fact) is the working memory. When an old friend tells you her new phone number and you hold the digits in your mind for a few seconds before writing them down, you are using your working memory.

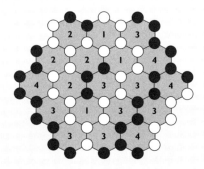

PUZZLE 10 Here is the completed Lighten Up grid. Smart Brain Action answer: Klrilg is (Hercule) Poirot, Nzikov is (Miss Jane) Marple, and Drnhvb is (Lord Peter) Wimsey, fictional detectives all. The code is a simple reverse alphabet code (A = Z, B = Y ... Z = A).

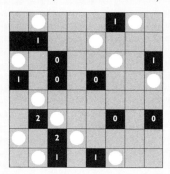

PUZZLE 11 Did you notice any benefit from the Ancient Indian techniques? Using repetition keeps your focus sharp on what you are learning, and as you proceed you test yourself and revisit what you are committing to memory, little by little. This focused circling progress is designed to drive the words deep into your consciousness.

PUZZLE 12 The completed grid should appear as shown below. You needed the top-right diamond clue to move from 1 to 2, then the diamond below that to move from 2 to 3—and so on.

PUZZLE 13 Easy = 9; Tough = 4. I always say to anyone who finds mental arithmetic difficult, "you'll notice the benefits of a little practice." It's not hard work to do a few number sums in puzzle books or to do day-to-day arithmetic in your head; persevering will improve your performance and build your confidence in using numbers.

PUZZLE 14 The full grid is shown above right, with each row, column, and long diagonal holding four different shapes and the letters A,

B, C, and D. The anagram answers are: Ingrid Bergman, Humphrey Bogart, and Claude Rains. The link is that they starred together in the movie *Casablanca*, famous among many other things for the song "As Time Goes By," with its line "You must remember this …"

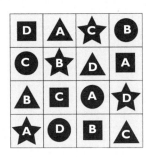

PUZZLE 15 To make the most of this technique, use all your powers of imagination to create memorable visual images for each place/fact. Try putting the exercise aside then returning to it after a few hours or a couple of days. You may be surprised how much fun the process is and how well you remember the facts. Feel free to substitute your own list for the list of "dem dry bones."

PUZZLE 16 The missing number is 3. With each Hub, add the light circles together, add the dark circles together and subtract the light total from the dark to get your central Hub number. Hub A light: 4 + 3 + 2 + 8 = 17. Hub A dark: 5 + 6 + 6 + 7 = 24 (24 − 17 = 7). The central Hub number is 7. Hub B light: 6 + 1 + 4 + 7 = 18. Hub B dark: 8 + 4 + 3 + 6 = 21 (21 − 18 = 3). The missing central Hub number should be 3. Smart Brain Action: 18.

PUZZLE 17 The answers are as follows.
1 5 • **2** Dark • **3** 2 • **4** 2nd in the 4th row
5 The 3rd • **6** A triangle • **7** 5 • **8** None
9 Yes • **10** 2nd in the top row

PUZZLE 18 i Limousine 2 to Garage B
ii Limousine 3 to Garage A
iii Limousine 1 to Garage C.
As an extra Smart Brain Action challenge,
can you remember one book or work by
each author? Or arrange the writers in
chronological order?

PUZZLE 19 The effect described by Proust
is well established but how well this kind of
sensory stimulation works as a technique for
learning and recalling things will vary from
one individual to another. Like most people,
I suspect, I find the sense of smell more
powerful than the sense of taste in this context.

PUZZLE 20 The completed pyramids are
shown below. Notice a pattern in the topmost
numbers? For an extra memory boost, cover
the book and see if you can write out the
completed pyramids. Answer to the additional
challenge: 28 + 24 + 23 + 29 + 16 + 16 +
20 + 22 + 24 = 202 (it is a palindrome, which
can be read in either direction).

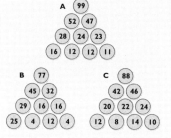

PUZZLE 21 The completed Neat Fit grid
is shown below. The two 9-square blocks in
the left-central and upper-left portion of
the grid make an intriguing place to start.
This type of puzzle is called a Shikaku. Try
practicing with free puzzles online; you can
also download free Shikaku puzzles to play
on your smartphone or tablet computer.

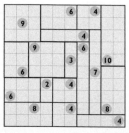

PUZZLE 22 Once you've rotated the
hexagons to match opposing faces, the
overall design should look like this. There are
a number of other symmetries in addition to
the one you've been asked to produce.

PUZZLE 23 There are fifty-six tiles in the
design: eight of them (a seventh) are white
and fourteen (a quarter) are dark purple.
Counting and then holding quantities in mind
while making calculations gives your short-
term memory a work-out.

PUZZLE 24 The poems of the English writer Thomas Hardy are good for learning/memorizing; many are available online and they often contain vivid characters and describe dramatic situations. Hardy was the author of celebrated novels including *Tess of the d'Urbervilles* (1891) and *Far From the Madding Crowd* (1874) as well as a prolific and intriguing poet. See Resources on page 143 for tips on finding poems online.

PUZZLE 25 The completed Number Nest is shown below: See, for example, that the dark hexagons at the top total 7 + 8 + 4 + 2 + 5 = 26, so 6 is the number in the central white hexagon.

PUZZLE 26 Say 4 is a hook on a wall, 7 an ocean liner, 3 a pair of bulbous eyes, and 2 a snake going down a staircase, you could imagine 4,732 like this: A hook is beginning to slip from the wall and will not hold the heavy picture of an ocean liner for much longer, but the young man with bulbous eyes does not notice because he is staring at the snake on the staircase. Smart Brain Action: The city of Dublin, through which the River Liffey flows: The third letter is B (right after A), and the fourth letter L (as in Liffey); the city is famous for the dark drink of Guinness.

PUZZLE 27 Check your answer against the Criss-Cross grid below. The 11 diagonal at the top left and the 6 diagonal at the bottom right provide easy places to start.

		11	31		27	12			
	6	4	2	1	8	7	9	3	5
	7	5	8	6	2	3	4	1	9
35	2	9	4	7	8	1	6	5	3	25
	7	1	6	5	9	4	3	8	2
22	8	3	9	4	2	1	5	7	6	16
	7	6	8	3	9	4	2	1	5
6	1	4	5	7	6	8	9	3	2	9
	5	3	9	8	4	7	2	1	6
	7	1	4	2	9	6	5	3	8

PUZZLE 28 How did you do? One of the benefits of this technique is that running through the facts one finger at a time amounts to an instant review of what you are learning. This is a key memory technique: Learn something, then review it a number of times at increasingly distant intervals. This enables you to fix the knowledge so that it is easier to recall.

PUZZLE 29 Each row and column in the grid should contain four light purple and three dark purple squares and two small white squares. A should be a light purple square, B a dark purple square, and C a dark purple square with a white inset, as shown.

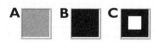

PUZZLE 30 A and D fit together to make a perfect cube. Puzzles that engage and challenge you in this way are good for your memory function. Smart Brain Action: $61,557 \times 2 = 123,114$, i.e. December 31 '14 • $861,570 - 761,459 = 100,111$, i.e. October 01 '11 • $791,091 \div 7 = 113,013$, i.e. November 30 '13.

PUZZLE 31 The answer, as shown, is David Bowie, creator of the album and single "Space Oddity" among many others. Bowie's real name is David Robert Jones. Reputedly he took his stagename from the American pioneer Jim Bowie.

1	3	4	2	1
D	A	V	I	D
			x	6
8	0	5	2	6
B	O	W	I	E

PUZZLE 32 Of course there's no right or wrong answer to an exercise like this. It's important to ensure you make a link between the narrative event/image and the item you need to remember; there's no point in remembering the story if you then forget what the individual elements are supposed to refer to.

PUZZLE 33 The completed Navigator grid is shown below, with all the letters in place in line with the given clues. The puzzle is an engaging test of logical thinking since you have to balance the requirements of the clues and so narrow down possible positions.

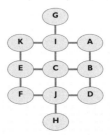

PUZZLE 34 Dark purple = left; white = up; mid-purple = down; light purple = right. The final die in your trip is the dark purple 3, fourth die in the second row. Logic and clarity of thought are key to good memory performance; being able to categorize information swiftly helps greatly both when learning and when recalling facts.

PUZZLE 35 As we've seen and as you'll know from experience, processing information into categories helps fix it in your memory.

PUZZLE 36 The new arrangement of the balls is as shown below. Like Dice Path (see Puzzle 34), the puzzle tests your logic in interpreting the clues.

PUZZLE 37 Fourteen revolutions of Cog A, which will make exactly eight revolutions of Cog B, and seven revolutions of Cog C. Smart Brain Action: $3 + 8 + 1 + 18 + 12 + 5 + 19 + 4 + 9 + 3 + 11 + 5 + 14 + 19 = 131$. Movies could be *Great Expectations* and *The Pickwick Papers*. Musical: *Oliver!*, based on *Oliver Twist*. Three other novels could be *A Tale of Two Cities*, *Little Dorrit*, and *Bleak House*. Edwin Drood: $5 + 4 + 23 + 9 + 14 + 4 + 18 + 15 + 15 + 4 = 111$.

PUZZLE 38 C2 is one-fifth of B1 (clue 10), so B1 is 20 (clue 5), thus C2 is 4. B3 is divisible by 7 (2), so B3 is 28 (7 and 15), D3 is 24 (15) and A2 is 12 (2). D1 is 3 (13), so A4 is 27 (4). A1 is 55 (1). C4 is 79 (12). No number is more than 99 (intro), so A3 is 52 (3). B4 is 13 (8). C1 is either 65 or 39 (9): If it is 65, there is no possible number for D2 (14); so C1 is 39. B2 is 50 (6). D4 isn't 78 (D2), so D4 is 77 (16). C3 isn't 27 (A4, above), so C3 is 90 (11). These answers are shown in the completed grid below.

	1	2	3	4
A	55	12	52	27
B	20	50	28	13
C	39	4	90	79
D	3	78	24	77

PUZZLE 39 The completed Shikaku is shown below. I find these grids make an enjoyable warm-up if I need to get my brain and memory function firing prior to writing or editing part of a book. Smart Brain Action: U.S. Presidents Ronald Reagan, Barack Obama, Bill Clinton, and Jimmy Carter. Can you put your memory to work to arrange them in the correct historical order?

PUZZLE 40 $A \times B = 170$. The numbers represent the number of sides in the shape they occupy, minus one. When shapes overlap, the numbers are added together. **A** $5 + 3 + 2 = 10$ **B** $9 + 3 + 5 = 17$. $A \times B = 170$.

PUZZLE 41 The number ladders answers are: Easy = 6; Tough = 19. For an extra challenge, devise four steps (one addition, one subtraction, one multiplication, and one division) to get from 6 to 19. Smart Brain Action: How about "Every adult must know English verbs?" *Here are the mountains:* Asia—Everest (Nepal/Tibet): 29,028 ft (8,848 m) • South America—Aconcagua (Argentina): 22,835 ft (6,956 m) • North America—McKinley (Alaska, U.S.A.): 20,320 ft (6,194 m) • Africa—Kilimanjaro (Tanzania): 19,340 ft (5,895 m) • Europe—Elbrus (Russia): 18,481 ft (5,636 m) • Antarctica—Vinson (Antarctica): 16,067 ft (4,897 m).

PUZZLE 42 Your images should be ones that catch *your* attention. Of course—as on page 43—there are no generalized correct answers. Here are suggestions: A shark ("Jaws" —George); the Sun (Sunil); a wrestler ("half-nelson") or Nelson's Column (Nelson); a plateful of food ("a meal," Amelia); a collar and tie (Taiwo); bags under someone's eyes ("eye sack"—Isaac); John Wayne (Wayne); surgical gloves ("germs," Jermaine); a car dashboard navigation system (from the Dutch TomTom manufacturer of these devices—Tom).

PUZZLE 43 There are fifty-two cells in the honeycomb: four of them (a thirteenth) are occupied by sleeping bees and thirteen (a quarter) are occupied by sleeping and wakeful bees. Smart Brain Action: I think St. Francis would not meekly allow an injustice; he would challenge the neighbor but allow him or her to keep the produce if in need. His main concern would be to be genuinely loving. Applying creativity to learning and recall techniques will boost memory performance.

PUZZLE 44 The completed Tile Align grid is shown below. This challenge is designed to get your neurons firing, maintaining and boosting the speed and accuracy of your thinking—which will have clear benefits for your memory performance.

1	2	2	2	2	1
1	2	2	1	1	3
1	2	2	1	1	3
2	4	4	4	4	2
2	4	4	4	4	2
3	2	2	3	3	2

PUZZLE 45 61. With each Hub, add the dark circles together, add the light circles together and then add the light total to the dark to get your Hub number. Hub A dark: $7 + 8 + 9 + 8 = 32$; Hub A light: $6 + 5 + 4 + 7 = 22$ ($32 + 22 = 54$); Hub B dark: $6 + 13 + 9 + 10 = 38$; Hub B light: $11 + 3 + 5 + 4 = 23$ ($38 + 23 = 61$). Smart Brain Action: 60 percent of 5 = 3; 40 percent of 20 is 8; 20 percent of 220 = 44.

PUZZLE 46 I expect you noticed that visualizing really helped fix the words in your memory. Visualization is a proven memory technique. It's worth persevering with it if you find it is not working for you straight away.

PUZZLE 47 Each row and column in the grid should contain four dark and three light squares and numbers that add up to 12. See the solution below.

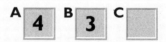

A **4** B **3** C

PUZZLE 48 The correct arrangement of numbers is as shown in the grid below. If you don't immediately take to number puzzles, you'll really benefit from working at them. Moreover, research has shown—as we saw on page 56— that working on a new skill or training yourself in a new activity benefits brain performance overall and the memory in particular.

		16	24		17	12		
	4	9	5	6	2	8	1	3	7
	7	8	4	1	3	5	2	6	9
22	3	9	2	7	4	6	1	5	8	27
	6	4	3	8	2	5	9	7	1
18	8	2	6	7	3	1	4	5	9	10
	3	7	8	1	9	5	6	2	4
10	5	4	2	3	8	7	9	1	6	14
	8	6	5	1	2	3	4	7	9
	7	2	3	6	8	1	9	5	4

PUZZLE 49 The layout below satisfies all the rules. In the top-right segment, for example, 3 + 5 gives the required answer of 8. I find this quite a difficult puzzle: Just as it is beneficial to confront yourself with unusual and challenging stimuli (see page 60), so it helps you to work at types of puzzles you find particularly difficult.

6	2	7	4	1	3	5
5	4	6	1	3	7	2
2	1	5	3	7	6	4
3	6	1	5	2	4	7
1	7	4	6	5	2	3
4	3	2	7	6	5	1
7	5	3	2	4	1	6

PUZZLE 50 See the grid below. Working this puzzle out demands concentration, patience, and the application of all your visual intelligence. If you're handy and enjoy making things, you may be pleased to know that research has shown quilting to be good for the brain and mental performance. Its social element is an added benefit.

1	8	7	■
■	5	2	6
9	3	■	■
■	4	■	■

PUZZLE 51 How did you do? This exercise usually demonstrates that revisiting what you have learned really helps you drum it into your memory. When I first did the exercise, I could remember all ten things after 10 minutes, but had forgotten two or three of them after an hour; yet once I had revisited the original list I was able to remember all ten items when I returned to the exercise after 2 hours. Smart Brain Action: 3 + 5 (= 8) − 6 (= 2) + 34 (= 36) ÷ 9 (= 4) × 13 (= 52) + 48 (= 100) − 3 (= 97) + 117 (= 214). To get back from 214 to 3: × 2 (= 428) ÷ 4 (= 107) − 104 (= 3).

PUZZLE 52 The completed puzzle is shown below, with each column, long diagonal, and row holding four different shapes and the letters A, B, C, and D. If you enjoy a social drink, the latest news is that it's good for you. Research in Mannheim, Germany, in 2011 indicated that older people who drank a glass of wine or pint of beer each day were 30 percent less likely to develop dementia.

PUZZLE 53 1 John Wayne—the "Ringo Kid" in *Stagecoach* (1939), Rooster Cogburn in *True Grit* (1969) **2** Jeff Bridges—Rooster Cogburn in *True Grit* (2010) **3** Montgomery Clift—Matt Garth in *Red River* (1948) **4** James Stewart—Howard Kemp in *The Naked Spur* (1953) **5** Clint Eastwood—"the Man with No Name" in *A Fistful of Dollars* (1964), *For a Few Dollars More* (1965), and *The Good, the Bad, and the Ugly* (1966) **6** Henry Fonda—Wyatt Earp in *My Darling Clementine* (1946) **7** Kevin Costner—Lt. John J. Dunbar in *Dances with Wolves* (1990)   Smart Brain Action: 16.

PUZZLE 54 The partition below works: there are six areas—of 2, 3, 4, 4, 6, and 6 squares, each containing two circles.

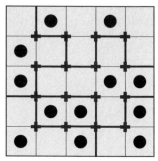

PUZZLE 55 The first button in the sequence is 2L at the middle far right, as highlighted below. In addition to the qualities mentioned on the puzzle page, this challenge requires (and develops) concentration and close attention. Both these are particularly built by regular meditation (see page 66). Smart Brain Action: $55 \times 2 + 30 - 4 \div 8 = 17$; $13 + 6 \times 4 \div 19 - 1 = 3$.

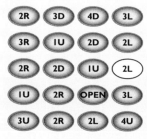

PUZZLE 56 The ships fit in the grid as shown below. If you have the time and inclination to do so, beginning to learn a musical instrument will bring you the brain benefits both of musical performance and of learning a new skill.

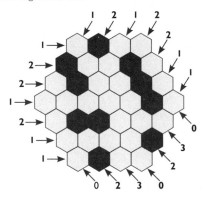

PUZZLE 57 This puzzle provides a great test of concentration and clarity of thinking. Cards total 87 (intro), so the 4 is missing—thus the 6 isn't card H (clue 3) and the 5 isn't card C. The Queen isn't card I (clue 3), so the Queen is card J (1), the 6 is F and the 5 is B. C isn't the King (3), so (2) the King is G, the 3 is H and the 8 of hearts is K. I and C are diamonds (intro) and A is a heart. E is a spade (3) and G is a club (intro). H is a heart and I is the ace (3). F is a diamond (intro). E isn't the 7 (3), so L is the 7. By elimination, cards D and J are of the same suit (intro), so D isn't the 2 (1). The 2 isn't C or E (3), so A. Cards D and L are of different suits (intro), so D isn't the 9 (4). The 9 isn't C (3), so E. C is the 10 (3), so D is the Jack. E is a spade (above), so L is a spade (4). J and D are clubs (intro) and B is a spade. *Thus:*

A = 2 of hearts, B = 5 of spades, C = 10 of diamonds, D = Jack of clubs, E = 9 of spades, F = 6 of diamonds, G = King of clubs, H = 3 of hearts, I = Ace of diamonds, J = Queen of clubs, K = 8 of hearts, L = 7 of spades.

PUZZLE 58 The answer is 154, reached as follows: 257 + 59 (= 316); 25% of 316 = 79; 79 × 3 = 237; 237 − 93 = 144; 144 + 32 = 176; 176 ÷ 8 × 5 = 110; 110 + 44 = 154.

PUZZLE 59 B and C fit together. Smart Brain Action: The missing numbers are 6, 10, 15, and 14. Each one- or two-digit number is the sum of the digits in the previous three-digit number.

PUZZLE 60 $68.60. There is one more circle and one more triangle in the smaller box on the right than in the smaller box on the left, so the difference in price is the cost of one circle plus one triangle, i.e. $7.80. Two circles plus two triangles cost a total of $15.60, thus two squares cost $5.60, so one square costs $2.80. The largest box contains one more square, two more triangles, and two more circles than the total in the two smaller boxes, and the two smaller boxes total $50.20, so the contents of the largest box total $50.20 plus $2.80 (one square) plus $15.60 (two circles plus two triangles). So the price for the items in the largest box is $68.60.

PUZZLE 61 **1** 5; **2** 4 dark purple, 3 gray; **3** 1; **4** 3; **5** 1; **6** 3 sunglasses, 2 regular glasses; **7** Yes, 1 in row 2; **8** Bottom row; **9** White; **10** Yes

Practice really helps with this kind of challenge, and exercising your short-term memory will make you better at noticing and recalling the kind of detail highlighted in The (Un)usual Suspects.

PUZZLE 62 The complete Number Pile pyramids are shown below. The puzzle is designed to build the speed of thought and numerical confidence you need when dealing with numbers in your short-term working memory. Additional challenge: The answer obviously varies depending on your birthday; in my case (birthday December 2nd so 1202) the top number of the pyramid would be 9.

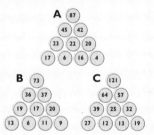

PUZZLE 63 If you convert the initial letters to numbers you get 1 2 4 7 7 7 13 19 20. A mnemonic could be Always Bravely Defiant, Great Green Giants Must Stand Tall.

PUZZLE 64 P—The value of the letter in the central square is half the sum total of the value of the letters in the other squares (A = 1, B = 2, etc.). Thus the missing value is 16, so the missing letter is P.

PUZZLE 65 The grid should look as shown below. Smart Brain Action: A = 62; B = 2,119.

PUZZLE 66 Once again, there are no right or wrong answers—the only thing that matters is that your rhyming numbers and the narratives or visual scenes in which you combine them are memorable for you. For example:

4,025: A poor (4) hero (0) come out of the zoo (2) alive (5). 7,963: I'm in heaven (7) near a pine (9), but my emotions mix (6) near any other tree (3).

PUZZLE 67 The completed diagram is shown below, with C due south of H, and H alongside B—and so on. If you haven't already read the book, I'd recommend *The Bellarosa Connection* (see page 79) for its meditations on memory and forgetting. The unnamed narrator, retired from a career as a memory expert, recounts the story of Harry Fonstein, a refugee from the Nazis in Europe who therefore had plenty to forget. As well as declaring that "memory is life," the narrator also likens forgetting to sleep and writes of "the roots of memory in feeling," which is relevant to our discussions of the involvement of emotions in remembering.

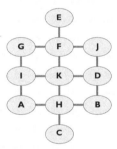

PUZZLE 68 See the correct arrangement of dominoes in the next column. You may read that you use only 10 percent of your brain power. This is a myth. It's true that you don't use all your brain at any given moment but over the course of, say, 24 hours you use 100 percent of your brain. Smart Brain Action: Mexico City is the odd one out because it is a city, and all the others are countries or in the case of Vatican City a sovereign city-state.

2	4	6	0	6	0	4
3	2	3	6	6	5	6
6	1	0	3	3	5	4
2	3	4	5	3	5	5
0	0	4	2	2	5	5
2	1	3	5	2	6	1
1	6	0	0	1	4	1
1	1	3	0	2	4	4

PUZZLE 69 Dark purple = up; white = left; mid purple = right; light purple = down. The final die on your trip is the white 2, fourth die in the fourth row.

PUZZLE 70 Twenty-four revolutions of cog A, which will make exactly twenty-one revolutions of cog B, twelve revolutions of cog C, and fourteen revolutions of cog D. Smart Brain Action: William Byrd, Ludwig van Beethoven, Benjamin Britten, Edward Elgar, Claudio Monteverdi, Wolfgang Amadeus Mozart, Jacques Offenbach.

PUZZLE 71 The completed grid is below. If you get stuck on a puzzle like this, it's a good idea to approach it from a different angle: Stop, perhaps take a break, then start in a different part of the grid.

7	9		5	1		8		3
	6	7		5	1	3	4	9
1	4		3		5		7	
	7	1	9	3	8	6		4
8	2		6		3		1	7
	1	8	4	6	9	7	5	
9	5		7		6	2		1
6		9		7	4	1	3	5
	3	6	1	2		5	9	

PUZZLE 72 A related concept is the mind map, originally developed by memory guru Tony Buzan. The mind map establishes clarity when you're processing information you want to remember, identifying key words and facts, laying out connections and linking related areas of knowledge; by processing the facts and establishing order in the mind map, you make it easier to understand and remember what you have learned. It also makes the information more memorable by engaging your visual sense. See Buzan's *Make the Most of Your Mind*, and *Age-proof Your Brain*, both listed in the Resources on page 143. Smart Brain Action: 61. First sum $24 + 25 = 49$, divided by $7 = 7$. Second sum $21 + 33 = 54$. $54 + 7 = 61$.

PUZZLE 73 i Car 3 to garage C **ii** Car 2 to garage A **iii** Car 1 to garage B

PUZZLE 74 The correct options are A and B. Visualizing in three dimensions used to be very difficult for me, but with practice I have raised my performance. Have you noticed any improvement after doing the similar puzzles 30 and 59?

PUZZLE 75 The grid below is complete. See, for example, A5 and A6 add up to 5, as in clue 1. It's a neat puzzle, isn't it?

	A	B	C	D	E	F
1	3	2	1	5	6	4
2	6	5	2	3	4	1
3	5	4	6	1	3	2
4	2	1	4	6	5	3
5	4	6	3	2	1	5
6	1	3	5	4	2	6

PUZZLE 76 Lines drawn on the Shikaku grid as shown below divide it into the correct alignment of rectangles.

PUZZLE 77 Certain facts are burned into our memory. I have a very clear memory of the answer to question 6 because we used to joke about my best friend's father's name. He was called Bob; and my friend would respond to people using the then-current phrase "Bob's your uncle"—meaning "then you're sorted"—by saying, "No he's not, he's my father." Other facts that you might expect to be able to remember are seemingly lost for ever. I have no recollection of the answer to question 1. I can visualize the car clearly—a Vauxhall Chevette. But I have no idea what color the seats were. Smart Brain Action: TZFTFRM = Gauguin, NRXSVOZMTVOL = Michelangelo, and NLMVG = Monet. The simple code is A = Z, B = Y, C = X, and so on.

PUZZLE 78 Look at the grid in the next column to see all twenty-eight dominoes in place. Domino Map is a variation on our Dominological puzzle (see Puzzle 68); both test logic, detailed attention, and spatial intelligence. Other factors that were found to help prevent mental decline and the development of

Alzheimer's disease (see Smart Brain Fact) were quitting smoking, controlling your weight, blood pressure, and diabetes (if you have it), and maintaining a positive attitude—keeping depression at bay. Trying to keep positive is good for your health in other ways: In 2011, research at Michigan University showed that people with a positive outlook were less likely to suffer a stroke and in 2010 findings at Columbia University, New York, indicated that people looking on the bright side were less likely to have a heart attack.

M	F	B	X	C	Z		4	2	5	3	1	6
X	M	C	Z	F	B		6	5	4	1	3	2
F	X	Z	M	B	C		2	4	3	6	5	1
C	B	X	F	Z	M		1	3	6	2	4	5
B	Z	F	C	M	X		3	1	2	5	6	4
Z	C	M	B	X	F		5	6	1	4	2	3

```
            6  6
         2  4  4  4
         4  1  5  3
   2  2  3  6  6  3  3  2
0  2  0  4  4  2  2  1  6  5
5  6  1  1  6  0  3  0  0
   2  5  3  6  0  1  3
         0  4  5  5
         0  4  5  3
            1  5
```

PUZZLE 79 GANDHI. $B + 5 = G$, $X + 3 = A$, $M + I = N$, $Z + 4 = D$, $F + 2 = H$, $C + 6 = I$. Mohandas Gandhi—widely seen as the "father of India" because of his role in the country achieving independence from British rule in 1948—is best known for his teachings on non-violent resistance. For a compelling insight into how Gandhi rose to such a height that he was called "Mahatma" ("Great Soul"), see *Gandhi the Man* by Eknath Easwaran. Gandhi himself declared, "I have not the shadow of a doubt that any man or woman can achieve what I have, if he or she would make the same effort and cultivate the same hope and faith." Smart Brain Action: Mnemonics for the seven deadly sins include "Wasp-leg" and "Peg's Law" or "We all see long elegant green plants."

PUZZLE 80 For other benefits of meditation, see page 66, and look in the Resources section (page 143) for a guide to the practice. Many other juices are recommended—see page 82 (beetroot juice) and page 96 (blueberry and purple grape).

PUZZLE 81 The completed grid should look as shown below. We recommend doing puzzles and playing mental games not only because they keep your brain cells primed but also because they are fun: Brain experts report that enjoyment and laughter are good for mental performance. If you have young children or grandchildren, try taking a leaf out of their book—see how they can put aside what troubles them and lose themselves in having fun. Smart Brain Action: He would have been 81; $81 - 53 = 28$.

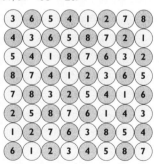

3	6	5	4	1	2	7	8
4	3	6	5	8	7	2	1
5	4	1	8	7	6	3	2
8	7	4	1	2	3	6	5
7	8	3	2	5	4	1	6
2	5	8	7	6	1	4	3
1	2	7	6	3	8	5	4
6	1	2	3	4	5	8	7

PUZZLE 82 On a memory walk or flight you will benefit from making the imagined scenes as vivid as possible. In this case, perhaps the truck is on the runway getting in the path of the airliner and the executive jet, or the horsedrawn coach, has collided with the tractor after losing control while avoiding a taxicab or a tandem in the farmyard.

PUZZLE 83 The numbers find their correct positions in the completed cross sums shown below. Any puzzle like this, which develops concentration and focus, will have benefits for the memory.

8	+	1	×	5	=	45
−		+		−		
4	×	9	−	3	=	33
×		×		+		
6	−	2	+	7	=	11
=		=		=		
24		20		9		

PUZZLE 84 **1** Months in decade (120) ÷ days in April (30) = 4. **2** Consonants in Mississippi (7) + vowels in Missouri (4) = 11. **3** Letters in Antarctica (10) − number of continents (7) = 3. **4** Minutes in a non-leap year (525,600) − seconds in a day (86,400) = 439,200. **5** Oars used in a rowing eight (8) + players in a soccer team (11) = 19. **6** Moons of Neptune (13) × planets in solar system (8) = 104. **7** Letters in "Internet search engine" (20) × consonants in "online security" (8) = 160.

PUZZLE 85 The completed grid is shown below. So if you were looking down the second column, for example, you'd be able to see a three-story, a four-story, a five-story, and a six-story skyscraper, but the one- and two-story buildings would be hidden.

6	3	2	4	1	5
5	1	3	6	4	2
3	4	6	5	2	1
4	2	1	3	5	6
2	5	4	1	6	3
1	6	5	2	3	4

PUZZLE 86 How did you do? If you want practice, why not try the card game known variously as concentration, memory, pairs, or pelmanism? This makes a good memory-building exercise. If you're not familiar with it, this is how you play: Lay out a whole pack of cards face down. Turn over two cards at a time: If they are a pair, keep them; otherwise turn them back over in the same place. You have to remember the position of the cards you have seen but not picked up, in order to gather in all the pairs. You can play solo or with two or more players, taking turns.

PUZZLE 87 D—The value of the letter in the central square is the sum total of the value of the letters in the top-left and bottom-left square divided by the sum total of the values of the letters in the top-right and bottom-right squares. Thus the missing value is 4, so the missing letter is D.

PUZZLE 88 The completed Battleships grid is below. For me the honeycomb arrangement makes this version of Battleships more challenging than one with a more conventional layout, because I find these ship alignments harder to visualize than simple horizontal/vertical groupings.

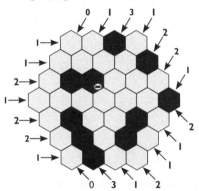

PUZZLE 89 The Numbercomb grid is shown below. Smart Brain Action: 12 + 12 (1) + 11 (2) + 10 (3) + 9 (4) + 8 (5) + 7 (6) = 69. Therefore, a refund won't be given because the train will make it 1 minute before the 70-minute deadline.

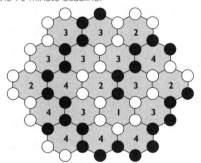

PUZZLE 90 1 The Virginian Hills casino **2** 11.06 **3** Ridgeview and Ninth **4** Heidar **5** Global Span Securities **6** 11.38 **7** Seamus **8** In a pouch worn around his neck **9** All in black with a blue mask **10** Anthony

PUZZLE 91 10. With each Hub, multiply the light circles together, add the dark circles together and divide the light total by the dark to get your Hub number.
Hub A light: $2 \times 3 \times 3 \times 5 = 90$
Hub A dark: $9 + 6 + 9 + 6 = 30$
Missing number calculation: $90 \div 30 = 3$
Hub B light: $3 \times 6 \times 5 \times 2 = 180$
Hub B dark: $7 + 4 + 2 + 5 = 18$
Missing number calculation: $180 \div 18 = 10$

PUZZLE 92 The A, B, C pieces are shown below: A should be a dark square, B a light square containing a 3, and C a dark square containing a number 1 button, as shown. Each row and column in the grid should contain four dark and three light squares, two buttons, and numbers that add up to 10.

A B C

PUZZLE 93 The path is shown on the shaded squares in the grid below. Further insight on keeping positive comes from the theories of Rosalind Picard at the Massachusetts Institute of Technology; she suggests that our state of mind can be measured on two spectra, one running from negative to positive and one from excited to calm. I find this can be a valuable insight when considering how positive I am or could be in a particular situation.

	99	51	16	7	14	54	70	21
40	63	54	35	39	91	92	26	72
21	92	33	81	75	84	80	36	98
7	99	98	49	67	35	38	18	31
45	30	20	22	24	99	94	35	18
91	14	77	90	42	9	68	97	27
35	34	70	73	23	76	81	63	77
36	96	51	93	27	54	28	26	14
41	84	7	21	42	32	97	65	74
42	28	25	37	29	84	36	70	56
66	81	49	63	90	56	69	95	

PUZZLE 94 The answers are as follows: Easy = 6; Tough = 30.

PUZZLE 95 The answer is 1,920, the process as follows: 631 × 5 = 3,155; 3,155 + 60% (1,893) = 5,048; half of 5,048 = 2,524; 2,524 × 3.75 = 9,465; 9,465 ÷ 5 × 2 = 3,786; 3,786 + 214 = 4,000; 48% of 4,000 = 1,920. The researchers on the benefits of working through the years around your retirement age suggest that you benefit from the stimulation of being in the workplace and of facing challenges. If no work is available, why not try doing voluntary work on a part-time

basis? Or you can get similar stimulation and benefits from joining an adult education class or setting up a book club or similar.

PUZZLE 96 See the completed Shining Example grid below. You should always feel free to work on puzzles with friends or your nearest and dearest. This brings more light to bear on a problem. Smart Brain Action: The road trip covers 1,138 miles/1,831 km.

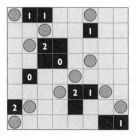

PUZZLE 97 The completed grid is shown below.

PUZZLE 98
1 One—the woman. 2 Six. 3 Phillies. 4 Two. 5 Red. 6 Three are wholly visible. 7 A door. 8 Leaning down. 9 Long.
By the way, if you look a little further in your online search you'll find some entertaining spoof versions of this iconic painting—including

one featuring characters from TV show *The Simpsons* and (my favorite) one with key characters from the Tintin comic books of Hergé. Tintin is the barkeep, Thomson and Thompson are the two male customers; a new figure (Captain Haddock, with Snowie the dog) looks on from outside the bar. Smart Brain Action: Andy Warhol. The code is a simple alphabetical/numerical conversion (A = 1 ... Z = 26) but with each letter moved on one place. So 2 is B (=A) 15 is O (=N) 6 is E (=D) 26 is Z (=Y) and so on. His painting *Eight Elvises* was sold for $100 million in 2009.

PUZZLE 99 The missing plate is D. Each row and column contains one center circle in light purple, one in mid purple, and one in dark purple. Each row and column contains one center star in light purple, one in mid purple, and one in dark purple. Each row and column also contains a total of ten white stars in the outer ring. So our plate has four outer white stars, a dark purple center, and a mid purple center star.

PUZZLE 100 The complete final grid is printed below. Smart Brain Action: The answer is 3. June, August, October, December is 30 + 31 + 31 + 31 = 123. January, September, and April is 31 + 30 + 30 = 91. May and November is 31 + 30 = 61. July is 31. Therefore 123 − 91= 32. 32 + 61 = 93. 93 ÷ 31 = 3.

								154
13	6	2	15	20	25	4	30	115
24	30	19	8	26	13	26	10	156
11	23	14	3	14	27	8	15	115
7	7	1	19	5	16	28	11	94
18	13	27	6	16	1	20	30	131
3	29	12	24	10	21	9	6	114
4	30	28	9	23	17	30	21	162
18	15	12	18	5	22	17	22	129
98	153	115	102	119	142	142	145	165

NOTES AND SCRIBBLES

RESOURCES

Books

Age-proof Your Brain by Tony Buzan, HarperThorsons 2007

Alex's Adventures in Numberland by Alex Bellos, Bloomsbury 2010

The Art of Memory by Frances Yates, Pimlico 1992

The Bellarosa Connection by Saul Bellow, Penguin Books 1989

The Checklist Manifesto: How to Get Things Right by Atul Gawande, Profile Books 2010

Delete: The Virtue of Forgetting in the Digital Age by Viktor Mayer-Schönberger, Princeton University Press 2011

Happiness: Lessons from a New Science by Richard Layard, Penguin 2011

ID: The Quest for Meaning in the 21st Century by Susan Greenfield, Sceptre 2009

Make the Most of Your Mind by Tony Buzan, Pan Books 2000

Memory by Alan Baddeley, Michael W. Eysenck, and Michael C. Anderson, Psychology Press 2009

The Memory Doctor by Douglas J. Mason and Spencer Xavier Smith, New Harbinger Publications 2005

Moonwalking with Einstein: The Art and Science of Remembering Everything by Joshua Foer, Penguin 2011

Passage Meditation by Eknath Easwaran, Nilgiri Press 2008

The Second Half of Your Life by Jill Shaw Ruddock, Vermilion 2011

The Secret Life of the Grown-Up Brain: The Surprising Talents of the Middle-Aged Mind by Barbara Strauch, Penguin 2011

See What I'm Saying: The Extraordinary Powers of Our Five Senses by Lawrence D. Rosenblum, W.W. Norton 2010

Stay Sharp with the Mind Doctor by Ian Robertson, Ebury Publishing 2005

Swann's Way by Marcel Proust (1913, first volume in *Remembrance of Things Past*, Penguin 1981)

Train Your Brain by Dr. Ryutu Kawashima, Penguin 2007

The Undiscovered Country by Eknath Easwaran, Nilgiri Press 2006

Use Your Memory by Tony Buzan, BBC Active 2006

Your Memory: A User's Guide by Alan D. Baddeley, Carlton Books 2004

Online literature

Bartleby: www.bartleby.com, for free books

Poets' Corner on "the other pages": www.theotherpages.org/poems

Eknath Easwaran: www.easwaran.org, for free meditation instructions and resources

143

THE AUTHOR

CHARLES PHILLIPS is the author of 30 books, including the best-selling *How to Think* series, published in 19 languages, and *Business Brain Trainer*. Charles has investigated Indian theories of intelligence and consciousness in *Ancient Civilizations* (2005), probed the brain's dreaming mechanism in *My Dream Journal* (2003), and examined how we perceive and respond to color in his *Colour for Life* (2004). He is also a keen collector of games and puzzles.

EDDISON · SADD EDITIONS
CONCEPT Nick Eddison
EDITORIAL DIRECTOR Ian Jackson
DESIGNER Malcolm Smythe
PRODUCTION Sarah Rooney

BIBELOT LTD
EDITOR Ali Moore
PUZZLE-CHECKER Sarah Barlow

PUZZLE PROVIDERS
Guy Campbell; Laurence May, Vexus Puzzle Design;
Charles Phillips; Puzzle Press